Arthur S. Link
Princeton University
General Editor for History

The American History Series
under the series editorship of
John Hope Franklin, *University of Chicago
and National Humanities Center*
Abraham S. Eisenstadt, *Brooklyn College*

Forthcoming Titles

Cover illustration: Courtesy District 1199, NUHHCE/RWDSU/AFL-CIO

Glenn C. Altschuler
CORNELL UNIVERSITY

Race, Ethnicity, and Class in American Social Thought 1865–1919

Harlan Davidson, Inc.
Arlington Heights, Illinois 60004

Copyright © 1982

Harlan Davidson, Inc.

All rights reserved

Library of Congress Cataloging in Publication Data

Altschuler, Glenn C.
  Race, ethnicity, and class in American social thought, 1865–1919.
    (The American history series)
    Bibliography: p. 114
    Includes index.
    1. Social classes—United States. 2. Ethnology—United States. 3. United States—Race relations.
  I. Title. II. Series: American history series (Harlan Davidson, Inc.)
HN90.S6A44   305.5′0973   81-17397
ISBN 0-99295-808-9   AACR2

PRINTED IN THE UNITED STATES OF AMERICA

82 83 84 85 87MA7 6 5 4 3 2 1

To Abe and Paulette, and to Bruce

EDITORS' FOREWORD

Every generation writes its own history, for the reason that it sees the past in the foreshortened perspective of its own experience. This has certainly been true of the writing of American history. The practical aim of our historiography is to offer us a more certain sense of where we are going by helping us understand the road we took in getting where we are. If the substance and nature of our historical writing is changing, it is precisely because our own generation is redefining its direction, much as the generations that preceded us redefined theirs. We are seeking a newer direction, because we are facing new problems, changing our values and premises, and shaping new institutions to meet new needs. Thus, the vitality of the present inspires the vitality of our writing about our past. Today's scholars are hard at work reconsidering every major field of our history: its politics, diplomacy, economy, society, mores, values, sexuality, and status, ethnic, and race relations. No less significantly, our scholars are using newer modes of investigation to probe the ever-expanding domain of the American past.

Our aim, in this American History Series, is to offer the reader a survey of what scholars are saying about the central themes and issues of American history. To present these themes and issues, we have invited scholars who have made notable contributions to the respective fields in which they are writing. Each volume offers the reader a sufficient factual and narrative account for perceiving the larger dimensions of its particular subject. Addressing their respective themes, our authors have undertaken, moreover, to present the conclusions derived by the principal writers on these themes. Beyond that, the authors present their own conclusions about those aspects of their respective subjects that have been matters of difference and controversy. In effect, they have written not only about where the subject stands in today's historiography but also about where they stand on their subject. Each volume closes with an extensive critical essay on the writings of the major authorities on its particular theme.

The books in this series are designed for use in both basic and advanced courses in American history. Such a series has a particular utility in times such as these, when the traditional format of our American history courses is being altered to accommodate a greater diversity of texts and reading materials. The series offers a number of distinct advantages. It extends and deepens the dimensions of course work in American history. In proceeding beyond the confines of the traditional textbook, it makes clear that the study of our past is, more than the student might otherwise infer, at once complex, sophisticated, and profound. It presents American history as a subject of continuing vitality and fresh investigation. The work of experts in their respective fields, it opens up to the student the rich findings of historical inquiry. It invites the student to join, in major fields of research, the many groups of scholars who are pondering anew the central themes and problems of our past. It challenges the student to participate actively in exploring American history and to collaborate in the creative and rigorous adventure of seeking out its wider reaches.

John Hope Franklin

Abraham S. Eisenstadt

PREFACE

This book, I fear, has fallen prey to what a colleague of mine calls "the iron law of historiography." The law compels every historian to assert: "It happened in the period that I study." The "it" that happened between 1865 and 1919, I will argue, was the laying of the intellectual foundations of the liberal state, where government played an active role in ameliorating social and economic conditions. This change, furthermore, was largely a response to the injection of racial, class, and ethnic issues into the political arena in an era of industrial growth and dislocation.

In the decade that followed the end of the Civil War, white Americans debated the nature and extent of government "protection" of emancipated blacks. The Thirteenth, Fourteenth, and Fifteenth Amendments to the U.S. Constitution seemed to promise equal rights for blacks, but would the government vigorously enforce them in the face of southern intransigence? Should government provide education and a land dowry to Negroes, who seemed ill-equipped to support themselves? A fear that government programs deadened initiative provided a reason, and in some cases an excuse, for the early abandonment of Reconstruction. Many whites believed, moreover, that the innate inferiority of blacks rendered them incapable of enjoying the fruits of democracy, even with the assistance of organizations like the Freedmen's Bureau. As the hope of "forty acres and a mule" turned to disappointment, some blacks turned to separatism as the only way to combat prejudice, while others turned to populism, which for a time combined a program of active government intervention in the economy with calls for racial fraternity. A racist counterattack helped destroy the populist crusade, and blacks failed to command the attention of most progressives in the years before World War I. In this bleak period, however, social scientists were laying the groundwork for an attack on racism by demonstrating that environment, far more than biology, was the key determinant of human capacity.

As Reconstruction faded from center stage, immigration replaced "the Negro problem" as the dominant "racial" concern of many Americans. Because many of the newcomers came from southern and eastern Europe, considerable sentiment developed in the Gilded Age to exclude these "alien races." Nativists, who often fused concepts of race, class, and ethnicity as terms of opprobrium for the "lower orders," called on government to regulate the flow of immigrants and to take a larger role in "Americanizing" those already in the country. By the twentieth century, progressive reformers insisted that government serve a different purpose: convinced that an unwholesome environment constrained immigrants, the progressives called for a limited program of social reconstruction that would give substance to the rhetoric of equality of opportunity. An active government, many progressives argued, could foster, not retard, individual initiative.

The presence of immigrant workers, strikes, and tenement-ridden ghettoes in the 1880s and 1890s were grim reminders that class conflict, usually defined as an uprising of the "lower orders," might plague the United States as it had Europe. The ideology of laissez-faire, newly clothed in the Darwinist language of "survival of the fittest" and "natural selection," seemed to say that because the plight of the poor was their own fault social classes owed little to one another. Amid the din of Haymarket, Coxey's Army, and the Pullman Strike, however, such language sounded smug and perhaps anachronistic. By the end of the century economists and sociologists had replaced Social Darwinism with new social theories that would be used by progressives to argue that a vigorous government, guarding individualism and equality of opportunity, could render class conflict as unnecessary as it would be destructive. The progressives argued that 1) rational planning and cooperation must replace unregulated competition; 2) responsible corporations and unions, legitimate organizations of industrial capitalism, should bargain with one another, encouraged if necessary by a neutral government; 3) toleration of other cultures (which progressives often subordinated to some form of Americanization) should be substituted for Anglo-Saxon chauvinism; 4) racial, ethnic, and class allegiances must be subordinated to civic and national loyalty. Respect, security, and prosperity would certainly promote harmony between the classes. Stability depended upon justice—and progressives believed that American abundance could guarantee both.

The progressive synthesis, despite an interruption for the 1920s "return to normalcy," dominated American social thought in the generations that have followed. The New Deal "broker state," for example, redefined liberalism by fully developing ideas which existed in embryo in the early twentieth century. If the Square Deal solemnly pledged special favors for none, New Deal pluralism promised special favors for all. Social thought in the 1980s, in fact, is still dominated, to a significant extent, by faith in orderly change and the productive friction of pluralism. Yet, as our faith in limitless abundance recedes, as our confidence in centralized planning by "big government" ebbs, Americans may well be ready for a new synthesis in social thought.

ACKNOWLEDGMENTS

This book has been enriched by the criticism of many colleagues and friends. The probing intellects and editorial expertise of A. S. Eisenstadt and John Hope Franklin forced me to refine and reformulate many of my ideas—and to extinguish unnecessary adjectives and adverbs. They are superb editors. Bill Brown, Ray Davis, Eldon Eisenach, Jim Hijiya, Hilmar Jensen, Peter Kardas, Marty LaForse, Paul McBride, Jake Ryan, Jan Saltzgaber, and Joe Tempesta read and reread all or part of the manuscript and listened as I thought out loud. Despite their stubborn refusal to accept blame for any errors that may remain in the book, I wish to thank them for their patience and their friendship.

In a book designed for undergraduates, it seemed appropriate to recruit some students to read the manuscript. Happily, my guinea pigs were sensitive readers and wonderful people. Todd Bernstein, Jed Horwitt, Eric Kotcher, Mark Lamphier, Dana Robin and David Sherman are answers to a teacher's dreams.

Lana Morse is far more than a typist. She is intelligent, unbelievably efficient, and I am honored to call her a friend.

My greatest debt, finally, is to my parents, whose influence on this book was indirect but profound. They taught a respect for individual difference and a reverence for human solidarity that seems so much a part of this book.

Glenn C. Altschuler
Ithaca, New York
June 1, 1980

CONTENTS

ONE

The Persistence of Race and Racism

BLACK AMERICANS

As the Civil War exacted an increasing toll in blood and death, Americans in the North strengthened their conviction that this was a struggle to free the black race. Only an altruistic crusade could justify the carnage. But in the aftermath of Appomattox, white Americans would have to define their responsibilities with greater precision. Did the nation's commitment end with the legal prohibition of physical bondage? Should the federal government provide protection and an economic stake for emancipated blacks? Could the United States, which could not exist half-slave and half-free, survive as a biracial society? What was the Negroes' place in America and could they be made to "know" it?

In the half century that followed the war between the states, blacks and whites formulated answers to these unsettling questions. Most whites believed that blacks were innately inferior, that racial antagonism could not be overcome, and that blacks, at best, must remain a subservient group in white society. Those most eager to provide equal opportunity for blacks were constrained by a belief, little challenged in the mid-nineteenth century, that government activity deadened individual initiative. Their ambivalence about federal programs contributed to an early end to Reconstruction. Former abolitionists hoped that talented blacks could prosper by dint of hard work, iron will, and educational opportunities funded by philanthropic Northerners. Painfully aware that the federal government had abandoned them, blacks responded in a variety of ways. Many grasped the paternalistic hand offered them by whites because it meant economic survival. For many of those who spurned subservience, the only alternative seemed to be separation. Again and again blacks tried to go it alone. Yet, ironically, black "enterprise" often stoked white resentment at upstart Negroes. Racism, white hostility to government programs to aid blacks, and limited resources among blacks themselves, precluded economic security or political equality, and reinforced the belief in the innate inferiority of the freedmen.

At the turn of the century, reformers attempted to break through this vicious circle. The populists, who challenged both laissez-faire and racial antagonism, were branded "nigger-lovers" and routed. Nonetheless their programs survived the demise of the party, and facilitated growing acceptance of government regulation of the economy. Many progressives shared the belief that social conditions and not biology bred poverty and ignorance, and that government had a duty to protect citizens against the oppressive environment. A far smaller number of these reformers asserted that truly equal opportunity would give the lie to the myth of innate black inferiority. Although few blacks benefited in the short run from progressivism, the movement did succeed in legitimizing government efforts to ameliorate social conditions, and in undermining the ideology of racism.

Although the Thirteenth Amendment abolished slavery, it did not change the racial ideology that had for centuries supported "the peculiar institution." White Americans admitted that eons of history and prehistory obscured the origins of race difference, but they insisted that invidious distinction was a palpable fact. Nineteenth-century science, moreover, legitimized white cultural chauvinism. Before the war, studies made by the craniologist George Morton and others "established" the inferior mental capacity of blacks. Some scientists asserted that differences were so great as to suggest separate origin of species. Worried that such interpretations contradicted Scripture, one Southerner argued that the Negro was created before Adam. The serpent in Eden, he conjectured, was actually a black gardener.

Studies undertaken during the Civil War confirmed the view that the black race was inferior. The U.S. Sanitary Commission measured the brain weight of whites and blacks to the disadvantage of the latter. The Commission also made the astonishing discovery that in height, weight, and head size free blacks compared unfavorably to slaves. Freedom seemed an actual detriment to blacks, while statistics on mulattoes showed that miscegenation caused physiological deterioration. Unlike Caucasians but like orangutans, scientists concluded, Negro brains stopped growing soon after puberty. Closer to anthropoids than humans, their outlook for emancipation was dim indeed.

In the decades following the Civil War Americans sharpened their racial axes with tools fashioned by Charles Darwin. Darwinism, as interpreted by Herbert Spencer and the American popularizer John Fiske, meant the survival of the fittest. Since Darwin had assumed that intellectual faculties varied among the races, his disciples labelled racial differences permanent and unchangeable. They scorned environmental influence as an explanation of inferiority and therefore dismissed as fanciful proposals to combat racial inequality through government agencies such as the Freedmen's Bureau. In *The Descent of Man*, Darwin predicted that the civilized races would exterminate and/or replace savage races. Freedom from bondage presumably would not stave off extermination.

Darwinism, then, as John Haller has shown (*Outcasts From Evolution*, 1971), provided a proof text for advocates of immutable race differences. Because evolution always moved forward, asserted scientist Alexander Winchell, the present Negroes were superior to their forebears. Negroes were probably not descended from Adam, but Adam from them. The conclusion that emerged from these hypotheses was abundantly clear to the anthropologist Lewis Henry Morgan: savages might advance with time, he admitted, but the progress of advanced races would widen the gap between them and primitive groups.

The "science" of race stimulated the hope of Negrophobes that the "Negro problem" would vanish as the black went the way of the dinosaur. The direct competition with whites resulting from emancipation, they argued, would hasten the process of extinction. Blacks did have large genitals and enormous sexual appetites, but infant mortality and venereal disease would counteract sexual prowess. Nature, moreover, insured that abused sexual organs became functionless. Physicians agreed that mulattoes could not produce past the third generation. The census, then, should reveal the passing of the black race. Imagine the shock of most whites when the 1880 census showed blacks increasing faster than Caucasians! The 1890 census, however, was reassuring as was economist Francis Amasa Walker's explanation that because many slaves had not been counted in early censuses, the increase was more apparent than real. In 1896

Prudential Life Insurance's statistician Frederick Hoffman insisted that blacks were a bad actuarial risk. Refusing to attribute decreases in black population to oppressive living conditions, Hoffman declared that innate degenerative tendencies could not be reversed.

Blacks, of course, could not be dismissed with a wave of the evolutionary wand. Some whites therefore concluded that they must be physically removed from the United States. Colonization, of course, was not a novel concept, and several attempts were made to revive it in the postbellum period. The entire nation would be whitened if blacks moved toward the equator, their natural habitat. As earlier in the century, colonization foundered in part because its proponents hesitated to enlist the federal government in the project. The precedent of such "interventionism," they believed, would be dangerous. Thus colonization depended upon private philanthropy, assertions that equality in America was impossible, and exhortations to blacks that their mission was to Christianize Africa. With few exceptions, blacks were unmoved by these inducements, and white Americans gradually recognized that Negroes would remain permanently in their midst.

Although they, too, often subscribed to the ideology of race difference, Radical Republicans were disposed to use the federal government to aid emancipated blacks. In 1865 Congress created the Freedmen's Bureau, an agency within the War Department, empowered to distribute food, clothing, and fuel to destitute blacks. The commissioner of the Bureau was empowered to divide abandoned southern lands into forty-acre plots and lease them to former slaves. A year later the Civil Rights Bill transferred the responsibility for protection of person and property from the state to the federal government. The Fourteenth Amendment protected this bill from timorous future Congresses by defining U.S. citizenship, prohibiting states from denying the privileges and immunities of national citizenship or depriving persons of life, liberty, and property without due process of law. The Radicals pushed this legislation through Congress, often over the veto of President Andrew Johnson, despite bitter protests that such federal interference violated states' rights and vitiated individual freedom.

Misgivings about the augmentation of federal power helped undo the majority of the Radical Republicans. The extraordinary emergency of Civil War necessitated legislative and executive activism, many argued, but in times of peace federal power must yield to states' rights, local option, and individual initiative. When Johnson vetoed the Second Freedmen's Bureau Bill, which would have extended the life of the agency and placed the civil rights of blacks under federal military jurisdiction, Congress failed to override. Perhaps more importantly, Congress failed to provide land for ex-slaves. Many Radicals agreed that federal seizure and distribution of land set an ominous precedent that could be used by the idle poor in the North. The failure of land reform, Kenneth Stampp has concluded (*The Era of Reconstruction,* 1965), probably made the defeat of the Radical program inevitable, because it restored Confederate plantation owners to power. By 1870 all but the most ardent Radical Republicans concluded that the government had done all that it could or should do to aid blacks.

During the 1870s and 1880s the Supreme Court adjudged that the federal government had done too much; The Court robbed the Republican legislation of much of its meaning. In the *Slaughterhouse Case* (1873) the Court narrowly defined the privileges and immunities of federal citizenship as the rights of access to ports and travel to the seat of government. All other civil rights belonged to state rather than national citizenship. A minority of the Court, soon to be a majority, argued that the intent of the Fourteenth Amendment had actually been to protect corporations from burdensome government regulation. For this reason, they pointed out, the framers of the amendment had deliberately used the word "person" (a corporation is a legal "person") as the entity to be protected. Other decisions provided massive loopholes to evade the Fourteenth Amendment. In *U.S.* v. *Cruikshank* and *U.S.* v. *Reese* the Court struck down the Reconstruction Act of 1870 which made it a crime to interfere with voting rights protected by the Fifteenth Amendment. The constitutional amendments, the Court declared, prohibited states but not individuals from interfering with the rights of citizens. In *U.S.* v. *Harris* the Court invalidated the Ku Klux Klan Act of 1871 on the same grounds. In essence the Court had adopted as law the dictum of social Darwinist William Graham Sumner: "stateways cannot change folkways." The nation's highest tribunal had rendered the federal government powerless to interfere with denials of the rights of black citizens. With scattered protests from Radical Republicans, the promise of freedom quickly became, in C. Vann Woodward's apt phrase, a "deferred commitment."

The Supreme Court's decisions reflected a consensus in white America, and former abolitionists turned from government programs to voluntary philanthropy to aid blacks. Evolution—for some the deliverer of the Negro's death warrant—might actually raise blacks to the level of white civilization. If time alone could bring reform, education was its necessary agent. Compulsion was unavailing in a world where change could be measured in millenia only. Where political action and immediatism were efficacious before the war, the schoolroom and gradualism were now the twin helpmates of the Negro.

Abolitionists, James McPherson points out (*The Abolitionist Legacy*, 1975), worked tirelessly to bring educational opportunity to blacks. Northern mission societies sent New England women to the South to teach blacks cleanliness and industry, as well as the three Rs. Schools at all levels, in deference to southern public opinion, quickly abandoned attempts to maintain integrated dining and faculty housing. The curriculum emphasized industrial education, because northern philanthropists like George Peabody and John Slater insisted that their money be earmarked for practical training. Since aid to education legislation perennially died in Congress and state allocation for black schools was woeful, abolitionists and blacks were faced with the choice of industrial education or nothing. Northern philanthropists were proud of the substantial inroads made in illiteracy, but the reformers knew that they were barely tolerated in the

South—and then only because industrial education left blacks economically dependent and politically impotent.

Three unchallenged assumptions constrained Northerners sympathetic to blacks: 1) race differences are rooted in biology; 2) individualism must not be sacrificed in the effort to aid any group; 3) government programs tend to erode individualism. These assumptions reinforced each other and strengthened the expectation that blacks would remain in the "lower class."

Although they deplored the stereotype of blacks as bestial, abolitionists agreed that Negroes were inherently different from whites. They employed a gentler form of racism, which George Fredrickson (*The Black Image in the White Mind*, 1971) has called "romantic racialism." Black docility, benevolence, piety, imitativeness, and musical talent, whites asserted, made them "natural" Christians. In fact blacks served as useful counterexamples to white rapaciousness. Fredrickson has persuasively argued that "romantic racialism" was often transmuted into a doctrine of inferiority. Uniformly passive traits distinguished the race, and abolitionists often labelled their charges lazy. Left to their own inclinations, they would in all likelihood squander their "natural gifts" in rhythmic reveries. Thus they must be constantly watched, if not by plantation masters, then by New England schoolmarms, who tempered their affection with a stern regimen. Romantic racialism trapped blacks in a cruel Never-Never Land, forever subject to the oversight of condescending adults.

If paternalism was the most generous alternative offered by whites, its practice was limited by the doctrine of individualism. The right of enterprising citizens to make their way unencumbered by institutional restraint had become a universal imperative in late nineteenth century America. Government attempts to mitigate the worst evils of industrialism by regulating wages, hours, or working conditions were vigorously denounced as insidious attempts to undermine private initiative. This view, as we have seen, helped convince Congress not to redistribute land, protect black voters, or provide federal aid to education.

Because government action was ruled out, paternalism became defined as voluntary, individual initiative. Americans rejected the relentless logic of Herbert Spencer, who scorned charity whether it was dispensed privately or by the state. The philanthropy of a John Slater, they believed, brought credit to the donor as well as opportunity to the recipient. By contrast, government programs squandered tax dollars while creating a class of paupers, with hands perpetually outstretched.

Although most Southerners denounced northern philanthropists and schoolteachers as carpetbaggers, proponents of the "New South" also embraced industrial education for blacks. These influential journalists, industrialists, and politicians saw, as C. Vann Woodward has shown (*Origins of the New South*, 1951) that northern capitalists viewed the South as an outlet for economic expansion. Mechanization could revolutionize the tobacco industry, the cotton mills, and iron manufacturing. The South also provided a market for industrial goods. Yet the instability of this section, which was plagued by federal troops, seething ex-Confederates, marauding Klansmen, and frustrated blacks, gave investors pause. "New South" advocates like Henry Grady and Henry Watterson sought racial harmony as a means to attract capital.

Grady and Watterson knew that by the 1870s little faith in the federal government remained in black communities and insisted that they were the real friends of Negroes. If blacks acquired industrial education and manual training, they could earn a decent living, while helping to build a modern industrial South. Grady, who never doubted white superiority in intelligence, character, and property, believed that the best way to mitigate racial animosity was not to hold out the false promise of equality, but to train and protect blacks in a well-defined society. The process, he boasted, was already well under way: "Nowhere on earth is there kindlier feeling, closer sympathy or less friction between two classes of society than between the whites and blacks of the South today." "The races meet," he continued, "in exchange of labor in perfect amity and understanding. Together they carry on the concerns of the day, knowing little or nothing of the fierce hostility that divides labor and capital in other sections." Government programs raised false hopes and dashed this natural harmony. New South paternalists offered blacks protection and a livelihood but exacted a heavy price: permanent dependency and subservience.

If New South proponents offered blacks a little when the alternative seemed to be nothing, they provided white workers the solace of racial superiority. Ever fearful of interracial alliances among the poor, which might prompt labor agitation and discourage northern investment capital, Southerners strove to keep the races apart. With more truth than he realized, Henry Grady proclaimed: "If this instinct [of race antagonism] does not exist it is necessary to invent it." The Negro, James Baldwin has written, tells whites "where the bottom is: because he is there, and where he is, beneath us, we know where the limits are and how far we must fall." Southerners created the myth of the Old South, an Eden populated by kindly masters and obsequious Uncle Toms who treated all whites with deference. Sharecropping, crop liens, and Jim Crow laws convinced poor whites that blacks provided a bottom to which they could not fall. Genealogy and the search for aristocratic heritage became the avocation of white Southerners of all classes. Racial affinity was a powerful elixir, and poor whites often outdid their more affluent cousins in demanding the rigid separation of blacks and whites.

Even the most courageous defender of racial equality, George Washington Cable, ultimately bowed to some form of paternalism. Twice wounded while defending the Confederacy, Cable subsequently became convinced that slavery was a moral evil and that blacks deserved the rights guaranteed to all citizens by the Constitution. Nonetheless he had little faith in the federal government. Cable joined his fellow Southerners in denouncing the "dreadful episode of Reconstruction." He devoted his life to advocacy of black civil rights as a spokesman for the "Silent South"; compulsory Reconstruction had been set aside, he announced, "and a voluntary Reconstruction is on trial." Cable's "Silent South" failed to materialize. He was publicly vilified, witnessed the enactment of Jim Crow custom into legal statute, and finally left New Orleans for Northampton, Massachusetts, in 1885—unsuccessful but unsilenced.

Cable begged Southerners to acquiesce in political and economic rights for blacks. The vote, he believed, was crucial because it conferred political power and enabled blacks to force the Republican party to provide funds for education. Not only did he fight against disfranchisement, Cable stood virtually alone among Southern whites in opposition to segregated schools, churches, and railway cars. Cable recognized that such policies were destructive to the character of aspiring blacks who wanted the best facilities available. Separate and unequal facilities were unjust and illegal; separate but equal facilities were expensive and unnecessary. In a sense Cable sought to enlist laissez-faire doctrine in the cause of civil rights by insisting that Southerners need not actively aid blacks but that they had a moral responsibility not to construct impediments to the free exercise of the privileges of citizenship.

Southerners pounced on Cable's program and forced him, albeit reluctantly, to accept race difference as innate. Integration, his antagonists sneered, led inevitably to race mixing. Cable gamely replied that equal rights under the law did not necessitate forced intercourse between whites and blacks, nor did he expect such intercourse to occur. Whites advanced a theory of irreversible race antipathy, yet they also hysterically predicted that mere presence in the same room would induce sexual union. Having found a contradiction, Cable sought to exploit it to win friends for integration: "There is much said about race antipathy. I believe in it more strongly than do the opponents of a mixed school system. . . . I have that confidence in the Caucasion race to believe it will preserve its purity without the bolstering aid of mass meetings or the expulsion of well-behaved children from the schools. . . ."

Cable's argument was more ingenious than convincing. He clearly believed that once blacks achieved political and economic rights, contact between the races would increase. Strategy, as he saw it, dictated that he keep his preferences to himself. Cable's compassionate and courageous prescriptions for the "Negro problem" provided a meaningful alternative to the apathy or intimidation characteristic of his countrymen. Voluntary compliance, won through appeals to American generosity rather than by government coercion, provided the resolution to the nation's racial dilemma:

Yes the black is inferior to the white. The almighty has established inequality as a principle in nature. But the lesson it teaches is magnamimity, not scorn. To apply the words of Coleridge: 'The great God who loveth us, He made and loveth all.'

Cable left the South in 1885, still hoping that blacks would one day receive equal rights but in deep despair over his misguided and even malevolent countrymen.

The frame in which whites cast Negroes severely circumscribed the response of blacks, who had expected that the federal government would stake them to freedom by providing protection and "forty acres and a mule." Seduced by Republican promises, they felt abandoned as Reconstruction gave way to black codes and the Ku Klux Klan. While many blacks drifted back to their old plantations, others defensively met white racism with black separatism. Calls for a return to Africa multiplied in direct proportion to federal indifference and southern intimidation. Black leaders who opposed separatism tended to accept the ideology of laissez-faire individualism in economics and to counsel blacks that self-help was the only way out of poverty.

The most energetic proponent of African emigration was Henry Turner, Bishop in the Georgia A.M.E. Church. Turner believed that God made distinctions "in the color but not in the political or social status of the human race," but as evidence mounted that color defined status in the United States, the Bishop argued that blacks would receive respect only if they operated their own government. If five to ten thousand educated, middle-class Negroes annually settled in Africa, they could bury forever the myth of race inferiority. The "black mission" to civilize Africa, thus had the additional advantage of proving the worth of blacks. The African "city upon a hill" might eventually purify the intolerant United States.

As the indifference of the federal government became increasingly apparent, the Bishop defiantly turned the ideology of race difference on its head. He taunted blacks who thought they could win acceptance by copying whites with a tart reminder of black superiority: "God is a Negro." When the Supreme Court struck down the 1875 Civil Rights Act, Turner redoubled his efforts to raise money for a steamship line to Liberia.

The black nationalism espoused by Turner, Edwin Redkey argues (*Black Exodus*, 1969), was significant far beyond the small number of emigrants. Lack of capital, discouraging reports about the climate and economic opportunities in Liberia, and frauds, rather than lack of interest, discouraged many from leaving America. Turner, moreover, did not recruit from the poorest classes because he deemed them unfit, and he was unable to persuade those he thought best suited to civilize Africa to leave their homes. In the 1920s Marcus Garvey would use the rhetoric of Turner but draw upon the seething frustration of the poor to build a massive black nationalist movement.

Black nationalism, nurtured on a diet of alienation and despair, resulted as well in attempts by blacks to resettle within the United States. If the federal government was unwilling or unable to aid freedmen in the South, blacks hoped it might provide land for them in the Midwest. When a petition requesting homesteads, signed by 98,000 people, failed even to elicit a response from President Hayes, several thousand blacks decided to set out for Kansas anyway. Their story, eloquently told by Nell Painter (*The Exodusters*, 1976), demonstrates that white "bulldozing" and federal government apathy turned the hope of interracial cooperation into the resort of black separatism. Tenancy and sharecropping, often economically less rewarding than slavery, black codes that limited travel and contact with whites, and intimidation and violence against black voters testified to the permanence of the color line. Many blacks saw no alternative to "lighting out for the territories." The Exodus was a grassroots movement of blacks who refused to be deterred by the promise that they would rise with the New South. They recognized, Painter argues, that the protection offered them by the "better sort" of whites was ephemeral. Yet, even more than Turner, the "Exodusters" came reluctantly to separatism. "Pap" Singleton, the venerable cabinetmaker, hoped to take his people to Kansas, organize separately to achieve equality with whites, then return to a chastened South that would be ready to receive blacks as Christian brothers.

Black nationalism, Frederick Douglass had come to believe, was a self-defeating strategy. Using separatism to combat segregation, the great black leader argued, constituted a surrender of equal rights by making blacks dependent upon migration. By the 1880s, in part prompted by his marriage to a white woman, Douglass articulated an uncompromisingly assimilationist philosophy that attacked segregation, whether imposed or voluntary. "A nation within a nation," he insisted, "is an anomaly. There can be but one American nation. . .and we are Americans." Vilified by blacks and whites, Douglass counterattacked by naming futile Negro policies: race pride, race solidarity, and economic chauvinism. "Our union is our weakness," he concluded.

A successful transition from slavery to freedom hinged on the active cooperation of the Republican party. As a celebrated abolitionist, Douglass had worked closely with the Radicals in the 1850s and 1860s and expected that a Republican-dominated government would guarantee equal rights under the Thirteenth, Fourteenth, and Fifteenth Amendments. Both within the councils of the party and outside, he was a persistent advocate of a strong Freedmen's Bureau and southern land redistribution. Recognizing that opponents of black rights often invoked laissez-faire and states' rights to stifle equality, Douglass nonetheless could not persuade Republicans that Reconstruction was politically advantageous. By 1868, when party strategists recognized that they could capture the presidency without the South, interest in black rights all but disappeared. Douglass, however, clung to the G.O.P. as the only hope, albeit slim, for blacks. After all, strict adherence to laissez-faire philosophy and "treason" during the Civil War characterized the Democrats, leaving blacks few options in the dark days of the 1890s. Before his death in 1895 Douglass championed labor unity and industrial education as President of the Colored National Labor Union, but this weak organization attracted few members, and Douglass often found himself issuing exhortations to hard work and enterprise in an age of accommodation and retreat.

At Douglass' death, Booker T. Washington had become the black champion of individual initiative. Born in slavery, Washington benefited from northern philanthropy in the person of General Samuel Chapman Armstrong, founder of Hampton Institute. Armstrong's ambitious young protégé quickly gained entrée into the homes and wallets of northern benefactors and became head of Tuskegee Institute, a black normal school in 1881. Washington brought Armstrong's philosophy of thrift, industry, and education to Tuskegee, urging students to work their way through school by tending the grounds and cleaning the floor. The quintessential self-made man, the black Benjamin Franklin, Washington asserted that success awaited other diligent blacks.

For years, as his biographer Louis Harlan has shown (*Booker T. Washington*, 1972), Washington claimed that the only solution to the race problem lay in an alliance between blacks and the white upper class. The Tuskegee Wizard, who had less reason than Douglass to expect aid from the national government or the Republican party, recognized that wealthy whites, north and south, exacted a price for their assistance. Blacks must accept subordinate status by being respectful and docile. Instead of railing against segregation, they must strive to make separate facilities equal. Taking the lead from his benefactors, Washington refused to support the federal Force Bill of 1890, which protected black voters from intimidation. Until blacks became self-sufficient, he asserted, the ballot was meaningless, while political militancy angered wealthy whites who supplied the jobs to pave the road up from slavery. Because he believed that blacks had no choice if they wanted to make any progress toward equality, Washington urged: "Keep out of politics, make any concession consistent with manhood."

A speech at the Atlanta Exposition in 1895 catapulted Washington into national prominence. He counselled blacks to remain in the South: "Cast down your buckets where you are." If blacks learned industrial skills and ceased agitating for political and social equality, they would inch up the economic ladder by making themselves indispensable to the New South. "The opportunity to earn a dollar in the factory just now," he said, "is worth infinitely more than the opportunity to spend a dollar in an opera house." Negroes, he reminded his attentive white audience, were not inclined to strikes or union activity. Repeatedly Washington had delighted Southerners by refusing to press for federal aid to education or to protest the disfranchisement of blacks. After a speech by a congressman calling for the repeal of the Fifteenth Amendment, he rushed from the gallery to shake hands and win a $500 contribution to Tuskegee. In 1899, pleading that the interests of Tuskegee might be adversely affected if he involved himself, Washington refused to denounce a grizzly lynching in which the crushed bones and sliced liver of the black victim were sold to a crowd of onlookers. At times Washington even implied that those guilty of rape deserved lynching. At the conclusion of the Exposition Speech the audience, to whom Washington's message signalled the acceptance of subservience, leapt to its feet and pronounced him the leader of the race.

Historians have argued that Washington was aware of the dangerous tendencies of his public utterances and so clandestinely supported court tests of southern discriminatory legislation to compensate. Nonetheless his rhetoric buttressed segregation and racism as it consigned blacks to the working class. At best he advanced a variant of romantic racialism. "We are a nation within a nation," he averred, accepting as fact what Douglass strove to deny. Humble by nature and training, blacks must help one another to overcome the laziness and docility of the race, without aspiring to intimacy with whites; "In all things that are purely social we can be as separate as the fingers, yet one as the hand in all things essential to human progress." Washington preached a gospel of wealth, but to many the sermon sounded like a hymn to soothe the Untouchables. The Tuskegee Wizard generalized from his own experience: through hard work and ambition, with the help of sympathetic whites, Washington had succeeded, to the point of invitations from heads of state. At the turn of the century, perhaps the nadir of race relations in the United States, few disputed Booker T. Washington's claim to leadership.

The intellectual odyssey of T. Thomas Fortune, editor of the *New York Age*, underlines the apparent bankruptcy of any program for black equality in the context of widespread racism and government indifference. Recognizing that the Republicans took the Negro vote for granted, Fortune proposed a new standard for political action: "Race first; then party." Yet the meaning of this credo remained obscure, given Fortune's doubts about the danger of race solidarity, his defense of intermarriage, and his prediction that the process of absorption promised the extinction of the African as an integral race type in the United States. To complicate matters further, Fortune asserted in his book *Black and White* (1884) that the "Negro problem" was part of a class struggle that could be resolved only with an interracial coalition of workingmen. With praise for the organizing tactics of the Knights of Labor, Fortune predicted:

The hour is approaching when the laboring classes of our country, North, East, West, and South will recognize that they have a common cause, a common humanity, and a common enemy. . . .When the issue is properly joined, the rich, be they black or be they white, will be found on the same side; and the poor, be they black or be they white, will be found on the same side.

Yet, to be sure, Fortune did not know how the issue could be "properly joined." His calls for union agitation, systematic state-sponsored programs of common school and industrial education, and federal subsidies for black land purchases echoed Frederick Douglass and went virtually unheard.

The hysterical public reaction to the Haymarket Riot of 1886, the replacement of the Knights of Labor by the segregationist American Federation of Labor, and the ever tightening grip of Jim Crow, convinced Fortune that the hour of class solidarity was not approaching. The editor's continual financial woes, Emma Lou Thornbrough adds (*T. Thomas Fortune: Militant Journalist,* 1972), forced him to mute his opinions to satisfy his principal financial benefactor, Booker T. Washington. Fortune had never seen self-help and joint action by blacks and whites as antithetical, but repeated rebuffs by whites convinced him to concentrate on black nationalism. He helped establish the Afro-American League, a precursor of the NAACP, and the National Negro Business League, designed to encourage black insurance, manufacturing, and transportation companies. Forced to live apart from whites, blacks must make a virtue of necessity by using their money to ease the movement of Negro entrepreneurs into the middle and upper classes.

Hostile to unions, Fortune now embraced the gospel of wealth of Horatio Alger, Andrew Carnegie, and Booker T. Washington. Black capitalism, he insisted, was a temporary expedient to be abandoned once it had demonstrated the dignity of the race: "When the lowly condition of the black man has passed away, when he becomes a capable bank president. . .his color will be swallowed up in his reputation." Yet Fortune did not confront the paradox of black capitalists delineated over a half century later by the sociologist Gunnar Myrdal: "On the one hand they find that the caste wall blocks their economic and social opportunities. On the other hand, they have, at the same time, a vested interest in racial segregation since it gives them what opportunity they have." Without the resources to be self-supporting, black capitalism could not employ many ghetto residents who continued to seek menial employment. The success of Negro businesses, as Myrdal suggests, was based on exploitation of blacks. The temporary expedient maintained a permanent caste, and the doctrine of race inferiority was provided with new evidence of its validity.

As blacks virtually abandoned hope that the federal government would help them, disgruntled farmers sought to enlist the government in agrarian reform. Dependent upon the railroad, the banker, and the vicissitudes of the international market, distressed at migration of their children to the immoral city, farmers in the South and the West combined to combat industrial capitalists. The world view of these Populists, who rejected both political parties as tools of the monopolists, was Manichean: the producers, farmers, and factory workers alike, were arrayed against exploitative finance capitalists. Because Populists did not deny the awesome power and influence of the enemy, they recognized that they must use their superior numbers to capture political institutions: only organized power could check the organized power of the moneyed class. The Omaha Platform of 1892 set forth the radical program of the Populists: government ownership of railroads, telegraphs, and telephones; a graduated income tax; currency inflation; a subtreasury system by which the government would store produce in national warehouses and give farmers credit up to 80 percent of its value.

A mass political movement in the South necessitated the inclusion of blacks, who constituted a majority of toilers in the cotton fields if not in the cotton mills. C. Vann Woodward has counted fifty strikes by white workers against Negro employment between 1882 and 1890—a testament to the ability of race consciousness to overpower class consciousness. Populists began to see that they had been duped. They supported efforts to end the convict lease system, a method by which blacks were arrested, often on trumped-up charges, and "leased" out to manufacturers, planters, and miners. Scoffing at the spectre of "Negro domination" forever conjured up in the region, the Texas Populist party elected two blacks to the State Executive Committee. Platforms called for an end to lynch law and the inclusion of blacks on juries. "It is in the interest of the colored man to vote with the white man and he will do it," insisted the fiery Georgian Thomas Watson. The "accident of color" Watson claimed, made no difference to the interests of small farmers, sharecroppers, and laborers: "You are kept apart that you may be separately fleeced of your earnings." Blacks and whites attended rallies together, jointly organized membership drives and appeared on the same platform.

It is possible, of course, to exaggerate the degree of racial harmony within the movement. Many Populists proclaimed that the United States was a white man's country, while others opted for segregated farmer alliances and labor unions. The central thrust of populism, however, made a few cracks in the color lines. The movement, as Lawrence Goodwyn has put it, contained a *Democratic Promise* (1976) because it held out the hope, albeit a slim one, of interracial fraternity.

The Populists mounted a serious challenge to Democratic control of the South in the 1890s. By arousing heretofore unorganized working people, industrialists of the New South and cotton barons of the Old South agreed, the new party might enlist state and federal institutions in social and economic reforms. The danger was clear—and the Populist alliance with blacks could be used to break the power of the People's party. Proclamations that the crisis approached in severity the horrors experienced during Reconstruction accompanied pleas that the South must be redeemed again or face the alternative of black domination. In appeals to white farmers and laborers to preserve the purity of the race, southern conservatives charged that Populist "nigger-lovers" supported blacks for elective office, opposed segregation, mixed socially with blacks, and evidently were not averse to race amalgamation.

While conservatives threatened Populists, they moved to minimize black support of the party. Many blacks were traditional Republicans who could be persuaded to remain with the G.O.P. When persuasion failed, force and fraud proved effective remedies: "I told them to go to it boys, count them out," Alabama Governor William Oates unabashedly confessed, in explaining his instruction to election officials to provide Democratic majorities in black wards. Populists were stunned as black votes apparently piled up for white supremacy. The race issue seemed to be chipping away at the white vote, without gaining substantial numbers of black ballots. By the early 1890s frustrated Populists attempted to bolster their racist credentials in hope of solidifying the white phalanx. The fragile interracial coalition had been smashed.

The career of Thomas Watson poignantly illustrates the lost possibility of the Populist crusade. Denouncing attempts to disfranchise blacks as "reactionary legislation," Watson had promised blacks that if they stood up for their rights, "if you stand shoulder to shoulder with us in this fight," the People's party "will wipe out the color line." But when he became convinced that the race issue would always prevent populism from getting a fair hearing, Watson threw his support to candidates who combined a Populist platform with advocacy of Negro disfranchisement. He spent the rest of his life denouncing Wall Street and out-niggering the most virulent Negrophobes.

After the defeat of the Populists in 1896, racists tightened their grip on the South. The cry of states' rights, which had been used to destroy Reconstruction, now justified the transformation of what had been custom irregularly applied into law in the statute books. State after state disenfranchised blacks often with the explanation that such action prevented Democratic election officials from stealing their votes. They sought, Woodward writes, to avoid fraud through fraud: literacy and property requirements, the grandfather clause, and the poll tax. This flimsy pretext delighted Democrats, who were only too happy to disfranchise supporters of the party of Lincoln. State legislation also carefully proscribed the activities of blacks in restaurants, parks, and on public transportation. In 1896 the Supreme Court put its imprimatur on "separate but equal" in *Plessy v. Ferguson*. The lone dissent of Kentuckian John Marshall Harlan ("Our Constitution is colorblind, and neither knows nor tolerates classes among its citizens") was dismissed as eccentric sentimentalism. The law seemed more blind than colorblind, as lynch mobs stretched it and the necks of their black victims. The popularity of Charles Carroll's *The Negro a Beast* (1900), which argued that blacks were biologically akin to apes, testified to the persistent virulence of white supremacy at the turn of the century.

Populists had lost the war, but in a very real sense they had captured the future. Within two decades most of their program passed into law, to be administered by an increasingly regulation-minded federal government. Interracial cooperation came more slowly, but the Populist insight that racism was a creation of economic, political, and cultural circumstances rather than biology gradually took hold in the twentieth century.

Although the first two decades of the twentieth century did not produce a dramatic improvement in living conditions for blacks, a few progressives attempted to breach the hitherto impregnable doctrine of innate racial difference. Convinced of society's responsibility in creating poverty and ignorance, these reformers believed that they had a moral duty to help raise the working poor and their families to middle-class respectability. As we shall see in Chapter Three, the progressives believed that providing equality of opportunity to all had the additional advantage of stabilizing a nation that had seemed on the verge of industrial conflict in the 1880s and 1890s.

The reformers borrowed from German-born anthropologist Franz Boas to explain "racial" characteristics. By demolishing any correlation among shape of skull, size of the brain, and intelligence, Boas cast doubt on the assumption that heredity accounted for differences between blacks and whites. He empirically demonstrated the fertility and physical vigor of race hybrids, laying to rest the notion that races were species, which could not interbreed. Citing evidence that a connection between race and personality had never been scientifically established, Boas attributed differences primarily to culture rather than race or heredity. White standards, the anthropologist pointed out, were used to judge other people. Thus the notion of the superiority of Caucasian civilizations was a tautology. Boas' cultural relativism, which he often applied inconsistently, did not gain immediate acceptance among social scientists, but by demonstrating that the very concept of "racial type," so unthinkingly used in America, was misleading at best, he had constructed a scientific launchpad for attacks on racism.

If society played a role in handicapping blacks (and immigrants), if poverty, not heredity, was the enemy, then society, through individual and government initiative, had a responsibility to equalize opportunity by providing education, minimum housing standards, and child labor laws. So argued a few progressive activists who established settlement houses, cultural and educational oases in the midst of the ghettoes. Centered in the urban North, the settlement workers ministered primarily to eastern and southern Europeans who often refused to frequent ethnically—let alone racially—mixed facilities. Ancient prejudices, combined with tensions created by job competition, prompted immigrant antipathy for blacks, and often resulted in segregated settlement houses.

Although they refused to force the issue with the immigrants, settlement workers spoke out on the origin and nature of prejudices. Henry Moskowitz, William English Walling, and Mary White Ovington helped found the NAACP. Two years later Ovington's sociological analysis of the Negro in New York City (*Half A Man,* 1911) attempted to break through racial stereotypes. The book was introduced by Boas, who admitted that the hereditary aptitude of blacks "may lie in slightly different directions" but denied that Caucasians possessed greater abilities than Negroes. Ovington agreed with Boas' view that equal opportunity for blacks was a myth. She saw race consciousness as the gravest obstacle to progress. An accurate measurement of the capabilities of blacks, moreover, was impossible in a society that confined the race to squalid housing, decrepit schools, and menial jobs. Blacks, Ovington concluded, were seldom evaluated as individuals because characteristics associated with the race were attributed to everyone. No one looked long enough to see a kindred but distinct and distinctive spirit. Ovington remained optimistic that exposing the irrationality of racism would weaken prejudice, a theme that characterized NAACP policy as well. Her insistence that environment shaped behavior and capacity, that nurture was more important than nature, signalled a reorientation of thought that would have profound consequences for blacks in the ensuing decades.

Although willing to expand the role of government in regulating the economy, most progressive politicians had little concern for black rights. The actions of Presidents Roosevelt and

Wilson epitomized official indifference to racism. Roosevelt entertained Booker T. Washington at the White House, then denied that he had broken bread with the Tuskegee Wizard when southern politicians raised their eyebrows at social intercourse between the races. The president appointed a few blacks to federal posts, but capitulated to racism by dishonorably discharging black soldiers faced with flimsily documented charges of rioting. Although he admitted that not all of the 167 servicemen were involved in the fracas in Brownsville, Texas, Roosevelt responded to "lily-white" Republican demands that he dismiss everyone. Noting that Woodrow Wilson expanded segregation in federal office buildings, Rayford Logan (*The Betrayal of the Negro,* 1954) argues that the southern-born president's record on black rights was even more dismal than Roosevelt's. "I will never appoint any colored man to office in the South because that would be a social blunder of the worst kind," Wilson candidly announced. Black rights were rarely a high-ranking agenda item for progressive presidents.

Although continually stymied by racism and economic oppression, black leadership in the twentieth century nonetheless spurned the Washington philosophy in favor of a more militant insistence on civil and political equality. Excluded from white organizations, especially unions, blacks, often defensively, retreated into separatism. Black institutions and white institutions stared uneasily across a widening chasm; interracial coalitions, the Populist experience demonstrated, were risky and fragile. Forced to go it alone, young black militants insisted that Bookerite obsequiousness be jettisoned in favor of a steadfast insistence on nothing less than equal rights, even though they knew that racial lines might tighten in the process. Although they were often willing to participate in the significant biracial organizations established in the progressive era, the NAACP and the Urban League, blacks chafed at the white monopoly on leadership and the glacial gradualness of a rhetorical and legal onslaught on racism. Progressivism frustrated blacks: its promise of equality and opportunity, apparently applicable to all citizens, spurred them to greater militancy, while the actuality of government indifference and economic exploitation bred anger and a sense of betrayal.

The most outspoken critics of Washington were William Monroe Trotter and W. E. B. Du Bois, two northern-born blacks who agreed that by refusing to fight for civil rights and accepting industrial education, blacks perpetuated their own servility. Du Bois hoped that a "talented tenth," properly educated, could demonstrate the capabilities of blacks, and help release their brethren from Sisyphean poverty. An all-black Niagara Movement, launched in 1905 by Du Bois and Trotter, called for suffrage and civil rights, free and compulsory education through high school, an end to Jim Crow and the discriminatory practices of labor unions. The vote was paramount, for without it blacks could not persuade politicians to commit the government to this program. Yet from the outset, the Niagarans lacked funds to disseminate their message. Isolated by their militancy and forced to denounce the color line from a financially shaky platform, the Niagara Movement died before its tenth birthday, testimony to the handicaps of a separatist strategy.

Race riots in Springfield, Illinois, in 1909 ignited a movement that resulted in the formation of the NAACP, a courageously interracial civil rights association, which adopted many of the goals of the Niagara Movement. The NAACP's strategy was to educate Americans to the effects of prejudice and to rely on the courts to protect black rights. Infused with progressive optimism, the association's leaders believed that the answer to the Negroes' problems lay in a massive campaign of public education that would ultimately alter the enviornment, erase prejudice, and render American law and practice truly colorblind.

The devil of racism, as NAACP members expected, proved to be extraordinarily difficult to exorcise. The reception accorded D. W. Griffith's film *Birth of a Nation* (1915) demonstrated that stereotypes remained fixed. Based on Thomas Dixon's rabidly racist book, *The Clansman,* the movie reaffirmed old canards about blacks and Reconstruction. The Negro at best was a thoughtlessly mirthful sycophant, at worst a rapist. The Ku Klux Klan was singled out for praise as the defender of southern womanhood in the otherwise lawless postbellum years. To insure success, the producers convinced Woodrow Wilson to preview the film. The president endorsed *Birth of a Nation* as historically accurate: "And my only regret is that it is all so terribly true."

The NAACP spearheaded a protracted campaign to ban this film, which gave authoritative sanction to racial degradation. Blacks boycotted and picketed theatres that persisted in showing the movie. The organization raised money to make films, using black actors, that would counter the pernicious Dixon-Griffith polemic. These efforts bore little fruit, but the organization refused to slacken its efforts. In a comprehensive history of blacks in American films (*Slow Fade to Black,* 1977), Thomas Cripps points to the drain on the resources of the NAACP, which viewed the film with obsessive hatred. The racist smokescreen kept blacks and their allies constantly off-balance, yet the struggle against Griffith's film brought the NAACP nationwide attention, attracted talented men and women to the organization, and began to create a climate of opinion less hospitable to segregation and more inclined to the belief that separate was unequal.

The effects of racial oppression occupied the genius of W. E. B. Du Bois, the only black leader (editor of *The Crisis*) of the NAACP. Educated at Fiske, Harvard, and in Berlin, Dr. Du Bois' work on the African slave trade and his brilliant sociological study, *The Philadelphia Negro,* launched a career that spanned seven decades. Racism, he wrote, exacted a toll in psychic tension as well as material deprivation:

It is a peculiar sensation, this double consciousness, this sense of always looking at one's self through the eyes of others, of measuring one's soul by the tape of a world that looks on in amused contempt and pity. One feels ever his two-ness—an American, a Negro; two souls two thoughts, two unreconciled strivings; two warring ideals in one dark body, whose dogged strength alone keeps it from being torn asunder.

Because he recognized that the demand for equal rights and the need for economic security often drove blacks in two directions,

Du Bois' attitude toward separatism oscillated. Black competition with white laborers sparked race prejudice, but the organization of a closed black business community had the same result. There seemed to be no exit for blacks. If they allied with whites, the latter expected them to accept subservient positions. With a few exceptions blacks could work for, but not with, whites. This very arrangement provided yet more proof that Negroes were helpless on their own. Black separatists, as the Niagarans had discovered, were labelled arrogant and ungrateful. Starting with severe handicaps, black capitalists frequently failed—more evidence of inferiority. Du Bois' anguish found expression in a simultaneous advocacy of "spiritual segregation and an economic segregation on the spiritual side," and physical integration.

Francis Broderick (*W. E. B. Du Bois: Negro Leader in a Time of Crisis,* 1959) has chronicled Du Bois' ad hoc attitude toward segregation in the years before World War I. He applied an economic test: separatism was justifiable if it demonstrably provided financial security. Economic survival meant that the Negro "must organize industry, that he must enter American industrial development as a group. . .and not simply as an individual, liable to be made the victim of the white employer" and white labor unions. The young socialist, A. Philip Randolph, taking such advice seriously, attempted to organize black workers. Rebuffed by white local unions and by the AFL, Randolph nonetheless nursed the Brotherhood of Sleeping Car Porters from an uncertain birth to a more robust maturity. Though president of an all-black union, he continued to fight for a coalition of black and white workers. Du Bois and Randolph recognized that separatists must practice extraordinary prestidigitation: even as blacks disappeared from view they must convince themselves and others that this was a temporary expedient, designed to render itself unnecessary.

Racism, Du Bois argued, was a "deliberately cultivated and encouraged state of mind," devised to keep blacks on the defensive, while dividing the work force. Increasingly Du Bois judged NAACP gradualism inadequate, because the association's program was epidermal: it barely scratched the skin of prejudice without treating the underlying economic disease. The virtual monopoly by whites of NAACP offices had ideological significance for Du Bois who exhorted blacks not to assume that "God or his vice [regent] the White Man" could do their work for them. Nonetheless, although Du Bois sometimes mused in despair that history taught that no human group ever achieved freedom without violence, he retained membership in the NAACP, which allowed him virtually independent control of *The Crisis,* a platform that could help him build "a new and great Negro ethos."

A few black artists and intellectuals acted on Du Bois' call for a "Negro ethos" that would bolster black pride by documenting black ability. Insisting that black culture had been, and remained, distinct and distinguished, they thought that celebration of it might reverse the defeatism that gripped so many. As black dolls and calendars appeared in the ghetto, blacks began to insist that they be called "Negro," rather than the more demeaning "colored." In 1912 Carter Woodsen founded the Association for the Study of Negro Life and History. The Association's *Journal of Negro History* provided a forum for the documentation of oppression and black accomplishment. Race leaders urged blacks to support filmmakers such as Oscar Micheaux and authors like James Weldon Johnson (*Autobiography of an Ex-Colored Man,* 1912). The roots of the "New Negro" of the postwar era, then, took hold before World War I.

The importance of the nascent black renaissance cannot be overemphasized. A veritable encyclopedia of achievement emerged, forcing whites to take heed and blacks to take pride. Yet black pride teetered on the precipice of separatism; testimony to human equality and dignity, black pride could turn to arrogance or hatred for whites. In the 1920s masses of blacks raced into the blind alley of Garveyism, rejecting polluting contact, while relying on a black capitalism that could not compete with its white counterpart. "Buy black" often meant spend more on limited choices. Black enclaves remained exploited colonies and the Back-to-Africa gambit a resource-draining pipedream.

As Nathan Huggins (*Harlem Renaissance,* 1971) has shown, the discovery of African "roots" mitigated the alienation of blacks. Yet, ironically, many blacks and whites had unequivocally supported assimilation because they believed that Negroes lacked any culture of their own. Thus no value clash clouded "the Negro problem" because, unlike immigrants, blacks were cultural *tabulae rasae.* The social critic Henry George, for example, contrasted blacks "with nothing to unlearn" to Chinese "with everything to forget and everything to learn." With the documentation of African and Afro-American traditions, however, ambivalence toward assimilation increased. To some, white civilization now threatened the integrity of black culture.

On the eve of World War I, blacks could point to few tangible gains in the half century following the Civil War. They remained mired in poverty and virtually imprisoned in ghettoes. Unions like the Industrial Workers of the World, which sought to recruit blacks and whites, found racism a formidable barrier. As if in answer to the call of *Birth of a Nation,* the Ku Klux Klan emerged from decades of hibernation.

Yet below the surface, faint tremors slightly shook the American soil. Although the ideology of innate race differences clung tenaciously on as reigning dogma, it had been shorn of its scientific sanction. For the moment local, state, and federal governments were deaf to the Negro problem, but progressives had moved tentatively toward altering the environment through legislation, a significant portent. The NAACP was preparing an assault on discriminatory laws that would restore the original intent of the Fourteenth Amendment. W. E. B. Du Bois must have retained some progressive optimism when he importuned blacks to "close ranks" in the war to make the world safe for democracy. If blacks shouldered their share of the war effort, white Americans might see the incongruity of granting them equal opportunity to die but not to live. Some blacks even petitioned the War Department to establish a camp for the training of "Colored officers for the Colored regiments." Although opposed to Jim Crow, they announced that "our young men are so anxious to serve their country in this crisis that they are willing to accept a separate camp.'' Black patriotism wrought no permanent changes, but in accelerating Negro migration to the industrial North, the war created new problems and new possibilities. Returning black soldiers were probably dismayed but not surprised to discover that the 1920s ''return to normalcy'' consigned them once again to the bottom of American society—a race apart.

NATIVE AMERICANS

The presence of emancipated blacks was not the only racial problem faced by nineteenth-century Americans. Indians, for centuries pushed west to make room for white settlements, now inhabited massive reservations on the Great Plains and the American Southwest. Relocated in these areas against their will, the Poncas, Navajos, Nez Percés, and Sioux remained in the path of miners, railroad builders, and settlers panting to enter the rich Black Hills. Despite the land titles held by Indian tribes and affirmed in perpetuity by numerous American presidents, these whites demanded that the federal government shove the Indians aside, or ground them under foot.

The inferiority of Indians was as little questioned as that of blacks. The Puritan view of the race as children of the devil persisted, justifying the frontiersman's dictum: ''the only good Indian is a dead Indian.'' Although they attributed Indian survival to the historical accident of isolation in the Western Hemisphere, many whites predicted that Indians would disappear rapidly when forced into competition with whites. Nonetheless, even if on the brink of extinction, the race could not be ignored, especially if the pace of American industrial and agricultural development was to be accelerated. So hesitant to ''reconstruct'' the South once some semblance of civil ''order'' had been restored, federal officials were inclined to regulate Indian affairs, which they viewed as part of the government's ongoing military responsibilities. Covetous Americans who expected aid from Washington in dispossessing the Indians found unwitting allies among vocal reformers who insisted on justice for Indians in the 1870s and 1880s but proposed to help by substituting individualism for communal, tribal values.

The reformers, middle- and upper-class men and women, were located exclusively in the East. Outraged at treaty violations that forced Indians from their ancestral homes, philanthropists and professional activists Peter Cooper, Albert Smiley, William Welsh, George Manypenny, Albert Meacham, and Helen Hunt Jackson formed the Indian Rights Association and the Women's National Indian Association to protect the beleaguered race. Apostles of individualism with affinities to John Slater and Samuel Chapman Armstrong, the humanitarians hoped to educate and civilize Indians to ease their entry into white society. Faced with a recalcitrant population, they pursued assimilation, often enlisting federal coercion in their behalf. The reformers' blueprint for Americanization in fact proved compatible with schemes to dispossess the Indians of tribal land, for in exploding the tribal nucleus, they left an atomized race, unable to coalesce or to fuse with white society.

Perhaps because they failed so dismally, the reformers have been harshly treated by historians. Whereas integration has often been the goal of historians of the black experience in America, it has been in disfavor among chroniclers of red-white relations for most of the twentieth century. One reason may be a sense among them that black culture had been destroyed in three centuries of slavery; western civilization would thus merely fill a vacuum. Because they thought that Indian traditions remained fundamentally unsullied by white intrusions, most historians have been uncomfortable with assimilation. The white reformers of the 1870s and 1880s, however, saw no way to preserve Indian culture without retarding the social and economic development of the United States. They opted for assimilation because they saw it as the last best hope for Indians, and because they believed that their own values could most profitably be adopted by all people.

The reformers were unashamedly ethnocentric. Franz Boas' research, devoted to Indians as well as blacks, was not published until the 1890s. Even the ethnologist Lewis Henry Morgan, one of the few to study native American life intensively, was not immune to the cultural chauvinism ultimately rejected by Boas' students. Morgan concluded that Indian hunters and herdsmen, unfamiliar with systematic agriculture much less industry and commerce, had not yet emerged from the barbarian stage of development. Indian communism and the "law of hospitality" impressed him: "I very much doubt whether the civilized world have in their institutions any system which can properly be called more humane and charitable." Yet he knew that these very traditions rendered well-nigh impossible assimilation into a society that worshipped competition rather than cooperation. Change might be effected in a few centuries, but time had run out. Lyman Abbott's forceful assertion reflected a national consensus that inferior races must give way before the inexorable advance of civilization: "Barbarism has no rights which civilization is bound to respect." American impatience left Morgan little choice because assimilation and isolation seemed equally impossible, given Indian culture and white appetites. Although he recognized that the consequences approached genocide, Morgan sided with his race; about the best he could do was to shed a tear at the funeral.

Despite the doubts of "Indian experts" like Morgan, reformers insisted that the American Indian could be made into the Indian American. The "savages" must be converted to Christianity and, just as importantly, an ethos of individualism must be inculcated into Indians long accustomed to communal ownership of land and deference to tradition and tribal chieftains. Indians, wrote Helen Hunt Jackson, must be made to "feel both the incentives and the restraints which an individual ownership of property is fitted to excite." Francis Amasa Walker, the Commissioner of Indian Affairs, agreed and was certain that government action was required to "snatch the remnants of the Indian race from destruction."

Like a wild horse the Indian must first be broken of bad habits, if necessary by the coercive force of the US Army. Dress, hairstyles, ornaments, and "superstitions" that bound warriors to one another, the reformers argued, must be discarded. Even more importantly, as Wilcomb Washburn has shown (*The Indian in America,* 1975), the Bureau of Indian Affairs implemented the policy of the reformers by unilaterally abrogating treaty provisions for annuity payments to each tribe. In the absence of buffalo and other game, driven away or killed by whites, annuities meant the difference between life and death. At the instigation of Indian Rights organizations, the Bureau decided to pay cash for individual labor, and thereby teach self-reliance. If the tribe no longer had largesse to dispense, Indians might be weaned from their allegiance to it.

The assimilation strategy was to substitute a Christian education for conformity to tribal customs. During the 1870s and 1880s denominational reformers, who dominated the Board of Indian Commissioners, replaced venal bureaucrats with dedicated churchmen as Indian agents for each reservation. These men, many of them Quakers, stressed individual salvation as they earnestly brought the Word to their charges. Rewards and punishments, they taught, came directly from God and not through tribal intermediaries like the medicine man. The proselytizers won converts, but because these new Christians only added one admittedly powerful deity to their pantheon, the reformers made no more than a small breach in Indian communalism.

As long as Indian youngsters remained in a "savage environment," many reformers concluded, they could not be effectively taught. Despite strenuous parental objections and numerous deaths from disease contracted in an unfamiliar environment, hundreds of Indian youngsters were sent to boarding schools in the East. Hampton Institute, so central to the career of Booker T. Washington, initially provided instruction in industrial skills for Indians. In 1879 the Carlisle School, founded by Army officer Richard Henry Pratt, took most of Hampton's Indian students. Pratt made no secret of his intention to force his pupils to change their ways: "In Indian civilization I am a Baptist, because I believe in immersing the Indians in our civilization and when we get them under holding them there until they are thoroughly soaked.'' In an effort to insure that the students learned the English language, Pratt mixed children from different tribes in the classroom. The English language served as the great equalizer, breaking down tribal traditions and blotting out the boundary lines which established distinct nations. Commissioner of Indian Affairs T. J. Morgan intoned that red men and women ''should be made to feel that the United States, and not some paltry reservation, is their home. . . . This civilization may not be the best possible, but it is the best the Indians can get. They can not escape it, and must either conform to it or be crushed by it.''

Loyalty to the United States and the efficacy of individual initiative were pillars of the Carlisle School, which convinced Pratt that Indians had almost the same intellectual capacities as whites (Loring Priest, *Uncle Sam's Stepchildren,* 1942). If they learned to compete, to guard jealously the fruits of their success, Indians could be released into the mainstream of white America. Massachusetts Senator Henry Dawes, the leading spokesman for reform in the political arena, summarized the aim of Indian education: ''[It] is to treat him as an individual, and not as an insoluble substance that the civilization of this country has been unable, hitherto, to digest, but to take him as an individual, a human being, and treat him as you find him.'' The implication was clear: shorn of tribal ''superstitions,'' armed with a trade and a Christian education, Indians would be productive citizens.

Indian reformers, unlike most of their counterparts in Reconstruction, insisted that the federal government must supplement education with a protected, individual title to land. Vigorously supported by the Indian Rights Association and Helen Hunt Jackson, whose *A Century of Dishonor* (1882) had indignantly catalogued the treaty violations of the federal government, Senator Dawes introduced a bill setting aside 160 acres of land for each Indian family and 80 acres for each single person. This red Homestead Act professed to provide Indians with a stake in society and an equal chance to compete with white farmers. Presumably the Dawes Act could be justified whereas the black request for ''forty acres and a mule'' could not, because Washington had wrought so much misery for Indians and the federal government had a responsibility to help repair the damage.

The Dawes Act of 1887, which governed native Americans until the administration of Franklin D. Roosevelt, was not, however, as altruistic as it seemed. First of all, the government had given the Indians nothing—except a small portion of their own land. More ominously, after each Indian received an allotment, the surplus land was sold to white settlers and the receipts held by the government in trust for the Indians. Fit enough to operate their own farms, Indians were not deemed capable of managing their own money. The amount of land disposed of in this manner is staggering. Henry Fritz (*The Movement for Indian Assimilation, 1860–1890,* 1964) estimates, for example, that the Blackfeet, Blood, Gros Ventre, Piegan, and River Crow of Montana lost 17,500,000 of their 21,651,000 acres. The beneficent face of the Father in Washington masked a greedy land-grabber.

The Indians had no say in the decision to sell their lands. Although Indian opposition to the Dawes Act, common knowledge to informed observers in the 1880s, was documented in a survey of Indian agents, a proposal to prevent the destruction of a reservation without the consent of a majority of the adult male population was eliminated by a House-Senate Conference Committee. The Indians recognized the validity of Theodore Roosevelt's claim that the legislation was "a mighty pulverizing engine to break up the tribal mass." Yet for this very reason, reformers who had chronicled America's "century of dishonor" as one hundred years of broken treaties now supported treaty abrogation on a scale more massive than ever.

Anticipating accusations that the Dawes Act was a thinly disguised eviction notice, reformers inserted several safeguards of Indian rights. The bill conferred U.S. citizenship on those Indians who opted for allotment, separated from their tribes, "and adopted the habits of civilized life." To insure that Indians did not precipitously dispose of their lands, the bill decreed that title was inalienable for twenty-five years. By that time, reformers hoped, education, citizenship, and the responsibilities of private property ownership would narrow the gap between the races and make Indians more capable of taking care of themselves. Further government assistance might well destroy the individualism that the Dawes Act was designed to promote. Believing that they had done all that they should for Indians, reform organizations self-liquidated in the years following the passage of the Dawes Act.

The safeguards listed in the bill proved illusory. Many reformers, Dawes among them, concluded that Indians were not really prepared for citizenship. The promise of citizenship was therefore withdrawn and wardship continued until the race gave greater evidence of progress. Even more importantly, when Congress in 1891 allowed Indians to lease the land they were forbidden to sell, hundreds of thousands of acres passed to white ownership. The vacillating attitude of reformers, unable to decide whether Indians were self-sufficient individuals or retarded wards of the state, made them pliable in the hands of cynical landgrabbers. Proposals that the Dawes Act scatter allotted land to facilitate contact with white farmers were rejected as too dangerous because isolated whites might be easy prey for reds. Severalty legislation left the Indians a beleaguered enclave, stripped of the support of tribal institutions, ill-equipped to survive as small agriculturalists. The reformers, who had expected most of them to fail, were sorry but not surprised. "Of course in many ways the Indians will be wronged and cheated," one sympathetic agent wrote, "but such a condition has got to be met sometime, and why not commence at once, instead of putting off the evil day?" Allotment provided opportunity for the best of the race—and only the best deserved to survive.

The reformers had genuinely anguished over injustice showered on the Indian, but ambivalences allowed economic interests to shape the policy of the federal government. The nation needed land—to promote agrarian development, to provide a safety valve for those discontented with industrialization, to facilitate the settlement of new waves of immigrants. Land fulfilled America's destiny, a nation spread from "sea to shining sea" but blocked by roving bands of savage nomads. Neither reformers nor the powerful arm of the United States government could extract Indians from the vice of history. The race, as the reformers saw it, faced two stark alternatives: "Join or die." Despite reservations about the possibilities of assimilation—sometimes based on racism, sometimes on an appreciation of Indian resistance and the profound chasm between red and white cultures—the reformers pushed ahead, prodded by corporations who sought to develop new markets (H. Craig Miner, *The Corporation and the Indian,* 1976) and railroad promoters eager to surmount tribal resistance to the granting of rights of way.

Indians saw removal to reservations and assimilation as two sides of the same coin: the buffalo was gone, replaced by a farmhouse sitting upon tribal soil. Responses to the white advance varied from resistance (often to the death) to acceptance by native Americans who policed their more recalcitrant brethren (William T. Hagan, *Indian Policy and Judges,* 1966). The impact of federal social policy on Indian perceptions is more difficult to gauge, given phenomenal tribal variations and a paucity of written sources. Indian culture, in any event, was not immune to the virus of American culture. An analysis of the Ghost Dance of the early 1890s may provide some insights into the narrowing range of possibilities for Indians intent on preserving their traditions.

Taught by a Paiute named Wovoka, the Ghost Dance religion prophesied the removal of whites from the world by hurricanes and other natural disasters, the resurrection of Indian dead, and a life free from want and misery. Wovoka called on all Indians to renounce fighting, to do justice to all peoples, in anticipation of the apocalypse. A ceremonial dance, repeated at periodic intervals, demonstrated knowledge and approval of the imminent event, which was to be accompanied by a return to traditional habits and native dress. The Ghost Dance religion spread quickly, albeit in widely different forms, to the Sioux, Cheyenne, Kiowa, Commanche, and other western tribes.

Wovoka's doctrine was remarkable because it predicted the

triumph of Indian culture amid a renunciation of active resistance to whites. Having exhausted most of their resources in conflict with the U.S. Army, many Indians could see no victory without divine intervention. Whites, after all, had violated sacred taboos by wantonly slaughtering game and desecrating ancestral homes. An Arapaho Ghost Dance song describes the plight of whites, left alone in the world by a deity bent on retribution: "We have rendered them desolate/We have rendered them desolate/The whites are crazy." White power had so overwhelmed red power that the only remaining hope was to invoke *deus ex machina*.

The Sioux transformed the Ghost Dance religion into a call to active resistance by claiming that the Great Spirit had sent whites to punish Indians for their sins, but the time had now come for deliverance from bondage. The "Ghost Shirt" worn during the dance, they asserted, also rendered Indians invulnerable to white bullets. The Sioux turned aside demands by Indian agents that the Ghost Dance cease. Their resistance culminated in the massacre of several hundred Indians at Wounded Knee, South Dakota, in 1890.

Both the militance of the Sioux and the passivity of Wovoka had their genesis in hopelessness. Both depended upon direct intervention by the deity, be it through a hurricane or a magic shirt. Indians had reached the court of last resort—and there is evidence that many of them knew it. The famous Sioux medicine man, Sitting Bull, the hero of Little Big Horn, when asked about the reaction of Indians to the Dawes Act, replied "Indians! There are no Indians left now but me." Although Sitting Bull recognized that the Ghost Dance flames that he fanned would end in death, he broke the peace pipe because he "wanted to fight and wanted to die."

The Ghost Dance aimed at keeping mind and body from assimilation, yet, ironically, its very ideology and ceremony borrowed extensively from white culture. The Ghost Shirt may well have been a refashioned Mormon "endowment robe." Even more significantly, the Messiah who would save the Indians was none other than Jesus Christ. The Kiowa ghost song, for example, rejoiced that "Jesus had taken pity on us." The call to Indian purity was uttered in white accents.

The Ghost Dance illustrates the paucity of alternatives left to the Indians. Two races, with vastly different cultures, shared the continent. Expansion, the internal dynamic of American industrialism, dictated that the Indian give way. White power, whether expressed in violence or relentless cultural transmission, would certainly triumph—and Indians could choose either a quick death with honor or individual survival amid the virtual disappearance of the race.

TWO

The Flame Under the Melting Pot

Two images vied for the minds of Americans in the century that followed the founding of the nation. One perceived the United States as an asylum which welcomed all victims of economic oppression or political tyranny. Individuals and groups in the pursuit of self-interest, James Madison wrote in the *Federalist Papers,* provided insurance against the tyranny of the majority. In the other image America was a moated fortress, the world's purest nation which had not been contaminated by the virus of

Old World values. Survival depended upon common goals, John Winthrop had informed his fellow Puritans, and upon a people "knitt together" by common ancestry and religion. For most of the eighteenth and nineteenth centuries these two images complemented one another because immigrants who came from northern and western Europe were predominantly white, many Protestant and Anglo-Saxon (the Irish-Catholic influx of the 1850s was a notable exception). Their quick assimilation seemed to confirm that an "invisible hand" directed the nation's settlement, facilitating economic and political freedom without loosening the cultural bonds of the republic.

Industrial capitalism and immigration, so obviously feeding on one another, raised disturbing questions for the future of America's unique balance of unity and diversity, individualism and conformity. Industrial capitalism seemed to guarantee *and* threaten equality of opportunity, liberty, and mobility. On the one hand enterprising Americans, free of government restrictions, had generated a productive capacity—and a standard of living—that rivalled any nation in the world. If immigrants clamoring to enter quickly discovered that the streets were not paved with gold, they also learned that they could vote, get jobs, and perhaps even think of someday owning their own homes, land, and businesses. Yet by the 1880s many Americans began to fear that by cramming thousands of low-paid, uneducated, and unskilled workers into factories and urban ghettoes, industrialism might be choking off opportunity, even as corporate monopolies strangled free enterprise. Individualism, equality, mobility—the conditions that had fostered economic growth—they believed, were imperiled by unrestrained industrial expansion.

The threat to American values seemed all the greater given the nature of the "new immigration" at the turn of the century. Southern and eastern Europeans, and Orientals, all wearing strange clothing and speaking a babel of tongues, streamed by the millions into the nation's cities. Yellow and swarthy, Catholic and Jew, often without knowledge or traditions of political participation, they were "alien races," probably incapable of exercising democratic citizenship. To many Americans, already bedeviled by blacks and the disruptions in community life brought by industrialism, immigrants heralded an imminent cataclysm. No longer knit together by religion, ethnic origin, culture, or even language, the frayed fabric of American society might soon be ripped apart by those who had little stake in the nation's "egalitarian experiment."

As Americans directed their attention to immigration in the nineteenth century, the concept of ethnicity and the relationship between government, individualism, and equality of opportunity were transformed. Many of the genteel class saw immigrants as fodder for vulgar and materialistic "captains of industry." Seeking to return to a golden age of cultural unity and deference to social position, they sought to exclude "inferior races," whom they thought innately incapable of understanding Anglo-Saxon values. To counter the power of industrialists—who welcomed immigrants as workers, consumers, and producers of profit—the genteel reformers turned to the federal government in the hope that the flow of immigrants could be regulated, or even shut off. By the twentieth century progressive reformers were prepared to use government for a different purpose. Armed with the belief that environment rather than biology constrained immigrants, as it did blacks, the progressives embarked on a limited program of economic regulation and social reconstruction. Government, once viewed as the foe of individual initiative, was now seen as a protector of freedom and guarantor of equality of opportunity. Because they sought greater cultural unity, many progressives tried to persuade, and even coerce, immigrants to "Americanize." Others hoped that respect for ethnic traditions would revitalize cultural pluralism in the United States. Despite these profound differences, progressives—far more than most of their contemporaries—often demanded equality of opportunity for immigrants, not only because it would guarantee stability and prosperity, but because it was just.

Centered mainly on the eastern seaboard, the genteel class bemoaned the materialism that pervaded industrial America.

Old values, manners, tradition, and art seemed lost in the scramble for the dollar, as the coarsely ostentatious noveau riche surpassed the genteel class in economic power and public esteem (Stow Persons, *The Decline of American Gentility,* 1973). If the genteel resented the crude manufacturers, they despised the new immigrants who labored in the factories. Barely literate in any language, apparently content to live in squalor, they symbolized the intellectual and spiritual decline of American civilization.

Genteel writers chastised immigrants for an inability to absorb Anglo-Saxon traditions. The "new immigrants," they insisted, could never learn the ways of the town meeting, the quintessential democratic assembly so characteristic of America. Conceived in the forests of Germany, transported to England and the United States, participatory democracy could be practiced only by the most advanced race. Nathaniel Shaler, a Harvard geologist, countered the pervasive idea that "a man is a man for all that! The truth is that a man is what his ancestral experience has made him." Peasants could be made into American citizens, Shaler taunted optimists, in about the same time it would take to mold an American into a peasant. When immigrants adapted to America, moreover, they invariably absorbed the worst habits of the populace. Charles Eliot Norton, professor at Harvard, pointed to immigrant emulation of American rootlessness, while Henry Adams, noting that Hebrew peddlers mimed Vanderbilt and Rockefeller, equated "Jew" with grasping capitalists. Always uneasy about the capacity of the masses to choose their leaders from the "natural elite," the genteel circle feared that naturalized immigrants would provide a majority for the mediocre or the unscrupulous (John Sproat, *The Best Men: Liberal Reformers in the Gilded Age,* 1968).

The genteel, Barbara Miller Solomon has shown (*Ancestors and Immigrants,* 1956), accepted the innate inferiority of non-Anglo-Saxon "races" as axiomatic. Like most of their contemporaries they tended to conflate race, national origin and character, social heritage, and biological heredity. Race mixing of any kind, they believed, produced degenerate offspring who would destroy American civilization. Charles Francis Adams, son and grandson of presidents, deplored the assumption implicit in the Declaration of Independence of "a common humanity . . . [and the] absence of absolute fundamental racial characteristics." Henry Cabot Lodge used Appleton's *Cyclopedia of American Biography* to prove that three-quarters of the nation's most eminent people had roots in England and warned that if higher and lower races mixed, the latter would dominate. Most agreed with E. A. Ross that southern and eastern Europeans were "the beaten members of beaten races."

If immigration continued many feared that the Anglo-Saxon race might perish. Francis Amasa Walker, the director of the federal census, pointed to the fecundity of the newcomers in comparison to the natives. While immigrants were going forth and multiplying, Anglo-Saxon families, because they saw the virtue of lavishing attention upon a few children, experimented with birth control devices. If current trends continued, the race might well commit "suicide" as "survival of the fittest" gave way to survival of the most.

By 1894 these fears gave birth to the Immigration Restriction League, which lobbied to compel the federal government to close "the unguarded gates" to the motley immigrant throng. The League did not emphasize the impact of immigration on the economy, but hints about a surplus of labor had special potency in the midst of the depression of 1893. The genteel class, self-appointed "custodians of culture," worried that immigrants could never understand the moral literature they wrote to temper the materialism of the age. Though small in number, League members sought to persuade Congress to make literacy a precondition for admission. President Cleveland vetoed the bill as an unwarranted exercise of federal power, but the League would be heard from again in the next century.

Because so many immigrants had already entered the country, restrictionists turned to the new science of eugenics to support their efforts to close the unguarded gates. Francis Galton, the English father of eugenics, labelled heredity the central determinant of human personality. Mental or physical defectives, criminals, and prostitutes, if allowed to reproduce, were likely to provide more deviants for society's care. The species could best be improved, eugenicists argued, not by the laissez-faire process of natural selection but by selectively breeding people, as farmers bred prize cattle and as Gregor Mendel cross-fertilized plants. The eugenics movement gained scientific respectability (Mark Haller, *Eugenics,* 1963) with the publication in the 1890s of August Weismann's experiments demolishing the theory that acquired characteristics could be inherited. In 1910 a Eugenics Records Office, headed by Charles Davenport, was established on Long Island to collect and assess family histories and to distribute material to eugenics societies throughout the country. Convinced that the government must act to prevent the reproduction of degenerates, the eugenicists succeeded in convincing fifteen states to pass sterilization laws before World War I. Several states banned intermarriages between "defectives." Davenport received congratulations for his efforts from public officials like Theodore Roosevelt:

Someday we will realize that the prime duty, the inescapable duty, of the good citizen of the right type is to leave his or her blood behind him in the world; and that *we have no business to permit* the perpetuation of citizens of the wrong type. [Italics mine.]

The popularity of the movement was clearly connected to immigration. Public officials and lay citizens believed that the ranks of criminals and idiots contained a high proportion of foreigners and blacks. Arrests and convictions reflected these prejudices, providing nativists with further evidence of inferiority. Oscar Handlin has demonstrated (*Race and Nationality in American Life,* 1948) that despite its own evidence that no correlation existed between the new immigrants and feeble-mindedness, crime, epilepsy, and tuberculosis, the influential forty-two volume Dillingham Commission Report to the Senate in 1911 took for granted the conclusion it aimed to prove: that the new immigrants were biologically inferior.

Proponents of restriction and eugenics were uneasy about immigrants because they were uneasy about their future in America. In a society that prized "unrestricted individualism," deference to "natural aristocrats" was in short supply. Elbowed out of power and influence by captains of industry, spurned by immigrants who preferred to traffic with urban bosses, the members of the genteel class despaired that they could counter the force of industrial capitalism (John Tomsich, *A Genteel Endeavor: American Culture and Politics in the Gilded Age,* 1971). Immigration restriction was an outlet for their crankiness, which was otherwise channeled into paeans to the cultural unity of the Middle Ages or speculations about the laws of civilization and decay.

The middle class, even more than the genteel establishment, had reason to regard immigrants with suspicion and alarm. As Robert Wiebe has argued (*The Search For Order,* 1967), the rapid pace of industrial change, punctuated by lengthy depressions in the 1870s and 1890s, disrupted and depersonalized community life. Controlled by economic forces they could barely identify, alienated middle-class people found order by joining organizations (the Daughters of the American Revolution, for example) that reaffirmed traditional norms, while providing identity and status. To such people, foreigners appeared as a threat to community homogeneity and economic security.

The fact that most of the newcomers were not Protestant, moreover, was especially chilling to Americans who, as Paul Carter has shown (*Spiritual Crisis of the Gilded Age,* 1971), were in the midst of a crisis of faith. The Roman Catholic Church was an especially mystifying force, akin to the corporation in its power, wealth, hierarchy, and authoritarianism. Josiah Strong asserted in the much-read *Our Country* (1885) that Italian immigrants were a huge fifth column sent to dominate the United States for the Papacy. The Catholic menace unified some Protestants by providing an external foe against which counterorganizations like the American Protective Association could direct their efforts.

In a sense these nativists, who believed that parochial schools, churches, and political activity proved the subversive intentions of immigrants, were more optimistic about assimilation than eugenicists. Little concerned about whether nature or nurture handicapped the newcomers, nativists insisted that the willful resistance of immigrants to Americanization could be broken. Staunch advocates of laissez-faire economics, they also strongly supported government activism in inculcating and regulating moral conduct. The fiercest battles of the era, Paul Kleppner has shown (*Cross of Culture,* 1970), were fought over conformity to Anglo-Protestant norms; such causes as aid to parochial schools, temperance agitation, and church expansion often found immigrants pitted against crusading Protestants. The American Protective Association (Donald Kinzer, *An Episode in Anti-Catholicism,* 1964) was only one of many Gilded Age organizations that lobbied for specific legislation to impose Protestant morality on clannish, ignorant foreigners.

Convinced that only public school attendance, mandated by each state, could ensure the transmission of the values of the community, most Americans insisted that immigrant pupils be taught the English language, Protestant prayers, and the catechism. School officials enforced truancy laws against families who persisted in sending their children to work, and championed legislation that compelled illiterates between ages fourteen and twenty-one to attend day or night school. The aim of educators, charges Marvin Lazerson (*Origins of the Urban School,* 1971) was to separate the immigrant child from the baneful influences of ghetto life. The teacher, a surrogate mother who taught structure through music, marching, and window-cleaning, insisted on obedience. Yet, although educators discouraged home visitations by teachers, their long-term aim was certainly to improve the child's home environment and prepare immigrants for citizenship by teaching language, hygiene, and principles of government.

The sympathy of teachers for immigrants often failed to overcome the expectation that they were destined for a life of menial labor. At first, the conviction of educators that the task specialization of industrialism robbed labor of its intrinsic value by depriving workers of control or knowledge of what they produced, led to prescriptions of manual labor for all students. Physical dexterity, they hoped—drawing on the philosophies of

John Ruskin and William Morris—would lessen alienation by teaching the older meaning of work: self-expression and individuality. (James Gilbert, *Work Without Salvation,* 1977.) The shared experience, moreover, increased sympathy between classes. As Henry Demarest Lloyd put it: "The manual training schools put the son of the millionaire by the son of the stoker at the forger and lathe."

Very soon, however, manual training became a parallel track for which most immigrant children were ticketed. Around the turn of the century, many educators turned to vocational guidance to facilitate job placement and satisfaction. By matching individual ability and employment in neutral, value-free aptitude tests, Harvard psychologist Hugo Münsterberg hoped to minimize alienation at work. In practice, however, aptitude tests institutionalized the biases of the evaluators, who were not surprised that immigrant children usually tested out as fit for unskilled labor. Vocational guidance, especially as "refined" by I.Q. tests developed in the twentieth century by Lewis Terman (reflecting his belief that environment counted for almost nothing in the formation of intelligence), did not escape the distinctions of race, ethnicity, and class it had been designed to overcome. The school pigeonholed immigrants as it prepared them for the world of work, while educators confidently proclaimed that aptitude tests enabled children to rise to the level of their ability.

Although the genteel establishment, the middle class, and their educational spokesmen reacted with discomfort and sometimes anger to the strangers in their midst, the anti-immigrant chorus did not always drown out other voices. Countervailing pressures, particularly the need for workers and consumers to fuel the economy, buttressed the tradition of America as a haven for all who wanted to come. John Higam's classic study (*Strangers in the Land,* 1955) demonstrates that attitudes toward immigration ebbed and flowed with changing economic conditions. Alternating waves of toleration and bigotry, unlimited immigration and federal restriction, roughly consonant with prosperity and unrest, swept over the nation between the Civil War and World War I. Ignored when times were good, the immigrant was often singled out for blame when the economy sputtered or the social fabric strained at the seams.

Preoccupation with the Civil War diminished interest in nativism in the 1860s, but the depression of 1873 and the labor unrest of the 1880s, which coincided with massive immigration, resulted in a widening wedge between workers, who resented job competition, and industrialists, whose control over wages and work conditions depended upon labor surpluses. Small business interests, represented by the National Association of Manufacturers, did not benefit from immigrant labor. They saw foreigners both as a boon to corporate giants and a threat to social stability. During the 1880s an alliance of small manufacturers and genteel reformers persuaded the federal government to assert its right to exclude immigrant paupers, mental defectives, and criminals. In 1882, largely in response to the agitation of Californian Dennis Kearny, Congress banned Chinese laborers for ten years and prohibited states from granting citizenship to Chinese. Six years later virtually all other Chinese were excluded. In 1885 the Foran Act banned the importation of contract labor. Although Charlotte Erickson (*American Industry and the European Immigrant,* 1957) has shown that only a handful of unskilled workers were recruited through contract labor, congressional debates indicated that proponents of the bill expected to exclude the "scum" of eastern Europe who glutted the labor market. The legislation of the 1880s did not impede the flow of immigration (except of Orientals), but demonstrated that nativists jumped when the economy pinched.

The response to the Haymarket Riot of 1886 illustrated that economic upheaval often spurred intense ethnic animosity. The arrest and conviction of eight anarchists (six of them immigrants) for bomb-throwing amid agitation to reduce the working day in Chicago to eight hours fused radicals, immigrants, and unions in many minds. Newspapers blamed the incident on "long-haired, wild-eyed, bad-smelling, atheistic, reckless foreign wretches, who never did an honest hour's work in their lives.'' The uproar contributed to the decline of the Knights of Labor. The American Federation of Labor, whose craft orientation meant minimal membership by unskilled foreigners, appeared as a "respectable" alternative to immigrant-radical-unions. Samuel Gompers, president of the AFL, did not join the protest against the treatment of the Haymarket anarchists. In fact he denounced radicalism and violence, and by the 1890s swung the Federation to support of immigration restriction, one of the few departures from its policy of noninvolvement in politics (Harold Livesay, *Samuel Gompers and Organized Labor in America,* 1978).

Anti-immigrant sentiments dominated the depression-ridden 1890s. The closing of the frontier, announced by the 1890 census and noted by historian Frederick Jackson Turner, limited the capacity of America to absorb foreigners and closed the "safety valve" of industrial discontent. "What in a few years more are we going to do for a dumping ground?" Henry George asked. E. L. Godkin, editor of the influential *Nation,* found "no corner of our system in which the hastily made and ignorant foreign voter may not be found eating away the political structure, like a white ant. . . ." Populist xenophobia, hinted at by Richard Hofstadter (*The Age of Reform,* 1955) and refuted by Walter T. K. Nugent (*The Tolerant Populists,* 1963), must be placed in the nativist context of the decade. With the return of prosperity in the early twentieth century, however, anti-immigrant excesses abated, and as we shall see, progressive reformers argued that the provision of equality of opportunity for immigrants was a key to social stability.

Nativism strengthened in immigrants the sense that they were "strangers in a strange land," and reinforced their inclination to live among "their own kind." Suspicious of government, which in the Old World was often synonymous with bureaucratic inefficiency or tyranny, the newcomers hoped that the American government would leave them alone to pursue their livelihoods and to join ethnic organizations that preserved familiar and honored traditions. Because they knew that economic necessity required acculturation, however, immigrants realized that their dilemma was not whether or not to "Americanize," but how and in what proportions to mix the old and the new.

In the novels *Yekl* (1896) and *The Rise of David Levinsky* (1917), Abraham Cahan poignantly described the attempts of garment district Jews to Americanize. The ability to speak and write English, to spout baseball lore, to dance were tickets to success with employers who favored "bright" employees. "Greenhorn" became the epithet flung by the newly initiated at those who were slow to conform. When immigrants gained economic security, Cahan lamented, they lost more than the trappings of their culture. David Levinsky cast aside the Talmud and desecrated the Sabbath in becoming a millionaire. Despite regrets over the world he had lost, Levinsky could not turn back.

Although they branded America a cultural thief, immigrants often recognized that changes were necessary and sometimes desirable. Cahan's advice column, the "Bintel Brief" (Bundle of Letters) in the Yiddish newspaper *The Forward,* Irving Howe notes (*World of Our Fathers,* 1977), willy-nilly informed Jews that their "landsmen" accepted New World ways. Numerous letters (often written by Cahan himself) asked whether Americanized immigrants should marry greenhorns. Other correspondents doubted that free-thinking Jews should attend synagogue just to please their parents. A housewife protested her husband's refusal to attend night school. Though expressed in Yiddish, the letters revealed an altered immigrant consciousness. Israel Zangwill's play "The Melting Pot" celebrated immigrant conformity to American nationality. Strangely attired foreigners stepped into a huge pot and emerged as clean, well-spoken, well-attired Americans. The shedding of Old-World cacoons became the measure of success and intelligence in the New World. Italians, Greeks, and Poles by the hundreds of thousands also changed, at first altering only externals— attire, speech—then slowly absorbing new values. Recent studies indicate that immigrant efforts were rewarded with a substantial degree of economic mobility. If rags to riches was a rarity, poverty to lower middle-class respectability was not, argue Stephan Thernstrom (*The Other Bostonians: Poverty and Progress in the American Metropolis, 1880–1970,* 1973) and Thomas Kessner (*The Golden Door: Italian and Jewish Immigrant Mobility in New York City, 1880–1915,* 1977).

While Immigrants absorbed new values, the American experience also heightened, and perhaps produced, ethnic nationalism. Immigrants often identified themselves at first not with their country of origin, but with their home town or region. They were primarily Sicilians, Neapolitans, Barians, and, only secondarily, Italians. The difficulty of life in the United States, movingly described by Oscar Handlin (*The Uprooted,* 1951), resulted in greater allegiance to the nation of their birth. Just as anxious natives found solace in organizations that promoted security through common identity, the newcomers formed institutions where membership was determined at first by town but very soon by nationality. Immigrants who had left their birthplaces spent precious dollars to guarantee that they would be buried among their countrymen. Nonetheless, immigrants frequently perceived no conflict in dual national allegiance. Each satisfied needs and desires; immigrants tried to define for each a sphere of influence.

Some definitions borrowed from sociologist Milton Gordon (*Assimilation in American Life,* 1964) may help explain how the immigrants balanced their allegiances. Gordon distinguishes between behavioral assimilation (acculturation) and structural assimilation. The former occurs when cultural patterns are changed to meet the needs imposed by a new society, while the latter comes about when immigrant groups are accepted into the institutions of the new society. Intermarriage is the most basic example of structural assimilation, which when complete means the disappearance of associations based primarily on ethnic similarity. While significant overlap exists between the two forms of assimilation, many immigrants sought acculturation without desiring or achieving structural assimilation. The melting pot, they believed, did not mean that they would become indistinguishable from the "Americans" that surrounded them.

Highly resistant to coercion, in the form of compulsory attendance at public schools for example, immigrants sought to control the nature and rate of acculturation as much as possible.
Acculturation facilitated individual social and economic
achievement, while resistance to structural assimilation promoted identity through intragroup activity. Immigrants sought
to have the best of both worlds.

Religious institutions were often the vehicles which regulated the process of acculturation (Timothy Smith, "New Approaches to the History of Immigration in Twentieth Century
America," 1966). Although Rudolph Vecoli ("Contadini in
Chicago: A Critique of the Uprooted," 1964) reminds us that
the connection of many Italians to Catholicism was tenuous at
best (Italians, a popular joke had it, attended church only when
"hatched, matched, and dispatched"), the influence of churches
should not be minimized. For immigrant Roman Catholics—
Germans, Italians, Poles—church membership weakened ethnic
particularism because it entailed subordination to a hierarchy
dominated by Irish prelates who often undermined old country
language and norms by exhorting their parishioners to Americanize. Archbishop Ireland spoke for many of his colleagues
when he endorsed Wisconsin's Bennett Law (1890), which required the teaching of English in all schools for a minimum of
sixteen weeks.

There were many, however, who insisted that cultural
homogeneity diminished religious zeal: "He who loses his language, also loses his faith." Most agreed that Americanization
was inevitable, but hoped that it could occur more gradually.
The removal of honored customs, they lamented, sundered the
family by creating generational conflict: "The melting pot
should not melt so completely as to result in something like a
porridge. . . . Rather it should be something like a goulash."
The traditionalists found a champion in Peter Paul Cahensly,
leader of a Catholic German Emigrant Aid Society, who charged
in 1890 that Americanization actually weaned Catholics away
from the Church. He proposed the establishment of separate
churches for each nationality. Priests should be of the same na-

tionality as their congregation and should conduct services in the mother tongue. Such a policy, Cahensly believed, provided a distinctive religious experience to counteract the lure of Protestantism.

The American Catholic hierarchy denounced "Cahenslyism" as dangerous obstructionism, primarily because decentralization shifted decision making and control of revenues to local churches. Church leaders saw the plan as a reversal of their efforts to remove the stigma placed upon the church as a "foreign, un-American" institution. Their lobbying activities in Rome resulted in the Pope's dismissal of Cahenslyism as ethnic parochialism, injurious both to the individual and the church. Although Rome frowned upon the establishment of national parishes, Catholic leaders assuaged conservative fears that ethnic differences would be obliterated. "Annex" congregations staffed with European priests of appropriate nationalities proliferated, so that by 1916 the Church contained 2,000 parishes that used foreign languages exclusively. All groups except the Italians set up parochial schools to teach English *and* the foreign tongue. Although the thrust of church policy supported Americanization, churches were at least semi-autonomous in regulating the rate of acculturation.

The Church carefully refused, however, to endorse ethnic pluralism. Parish property remained diocesan rather than ethnic, and prelates pronounced annex congregations temporary expedients to ease the transition of immigrants. At religious conventions, where few Polish clerics supported Father Kruszka's call for ethnic pluralism within Roman Catholicism, the call remained the same: "God first, then country" (Victor Greene, *For God and Country: The Rise of Polish and Lithuanian Ethnic Consciousness in America 1860–1915,* 1975). Amid the intense nationalism of World War I, as Richard Linkh has shown (*American Catholicism and European Immigrants,* 1975), advocates of ethnic pluralism received serious setbacks. Suggestions that European priests be Americanized for a year, then released to the parish, met with favorable responses. Ethnic parishes and foreign language schools, the argument now went, stifled the normal learning process of the second generation: "English is in the air; children born in this country drink it in with their milk." The antiforeign prejudice brought by the war served as an excuse and a prod for the church to move in a direction in had already charted for itself. Catholic leaders consistently and sincerely denounced Americanization by force-feeding, but many prelates strove to plan the cultural diet of their parishioners.

If ethnic exclusivity and fervid Americanization were poles that attracted some immigrant churchgoers, most viewed religious institutions as "sanctuaries in which individuals can find cultural comfort, but which also encourage them to use their abilities in the wider society" (Victor Greene, "Becoming American: The Role of Ethnic Leaders—Swedes, Poles, Italians, and Jews," 1978). Suspicious of outsiders, fearful of legislation that attacked their schools, churches, and saloons, yet anxious to learn the ways of their adopted country, immigrants turned to "cultural brokers" like the Swedish Reverend Tufve Hasselquist, the Polish Reverend Wicenty Barzynski, and the orthodox Jewish layman Kasriel Sarasohn. These "traditional progressives," Greene argues, urged their people to segregate themselves physically from the general society and even to educate themselves; but they also insisted that immigrants immerse themselves in American political and economic life. Hasselquist, who beseeched his Lutheran parishoners to understand political controversies and vote, also advocated abandonment of the Swedish language. Although Barzynski feared that Poles might "drown in the Anglo-Saxon Protestant sea," his major objective was to integrate them into the American Catholic Church. Polish atheists or nationalists who had abandoned the faith, he believed, were the greatest menace. Sarasohn retained his orthodox faith, but exhorted Jews to learn the English language and mobilize politically. The activities of these religious leaders and others like them, Greene and Milton Gordon agree, facilitated acculturation across ethnic boundaries, while strengthening immigrant communities and social networks.

At work immigrants had no mediators to regulate acculturation, yet the superb scholarship of Herbert Gutman (*Work,*

Culture and Society, 1976) no longer permits us to see this process, even in the factory, as easy or entirely successful. Gutman shows that the immigrant sense of time, for example, conformed to a preindustrial clock, which measured work by task rather than time. Placed in factories, immigrants struggled to make new conditions compatible with old assumptions without yielding artisan habits and pleasures. Slavic, Italian, and Jewish immigrants celebrated festivals even when they did not fall on Sunday. Cigar makers had newspapers read to them and struck in Milwaukee in 1882 for permission to leave the factory without the foreman's consent. Immigrants often worked hard, then took several days off, or even quit their jobs in protest against industrial conditions (Tamara Hareven, "The Laborers of Manchester, New Hampshire: The Role of Family and Ethnicity in Adjustment to Industrial Life," 1975), complainng: "too much noise," "too much dust," "work too hard." Immigrants often convinced employers to permit ethnic clusters in workrooms. Italians preferred outdoor construction work because it was more congenial to their Old-World patterns. Outside the workplace, immigrants also sought to retain the old ways. In 1902, for example, the Jews of New York City demanded that a rabbi set the price of kosher meat as in eastern European "shtetl." The flame under the melting pot did not so easily burn off the culture of the immigrants.

Still, despite the tenacity with which immigrants sought to stretch the system to fit their traditions, they eventually had to accommodate themselves to industrialism—or leave. Indeed, enormous numbers departed America, some as economic failures, some successful enough to purchase land in the old country. For every one hundred southern and eastern Europeans that arrived between 1908–1910, forty-four made the return trip. The outbreak of World War I, however, made the already expensive and difficult return to Europe well-nigh impossible. Those who remained acclimated themselves, albeit slowly, through increased contact with those outside their ethnic group at work and at union meetings. They had to, a Polish immigrant boy admitted: "We must be very attentive in our work, every hour, because if anything is bad, we are without work." Tamara Hareven notes that leaving the job decreased economic mobility and that Poles and Greeks were more attached to the mills than French Canadians, who could more easily return to familiar surroundings. A subordinate class, motivated in part by fear and in part by hope, immigrants could not escape the pressure of their employment, nor could they avoid carrying home the habits they acquired.

The tendency of immigrants to rely on fraternal, religious, and political organizations to regulate acculturation was typically American in its reliance on *voluntary* union with the like-minded. Like many nineteenth-century "sons and daughters of the American Revolution," immigrants saw no contradiction in the simultaneous pursuit of ethnic solidarity, economic individualism, and American values. Thus Donald Cole (*Immigrant City: Lawrence, Massachusetts, 1845–1921,* 1963) has found that immigrants found "security in groups" *and* "security in Americanism." Most immigrants, Timothy Smith reminds us, saw ethnic community not as a room but a corridor because it provided psychological and sometimes material sustenance that helped them sally forth in the wider world.

At first ethnic organizations provided services that would otherwise not be available to immigrants. Italian societies typically offered sickness, accident, and funeral benefits; society doctors and lawyers looked after the needs of members. Social and recreational facilities appeared in the midst of ghettoes. With few exceptions, however, immigrant groups, like blacks, did not develop economic institutions capable of sustaining the community (the Chinese, perhaps because of the intense racial antagonism they faced, had to be more economically self-sufficient and consequently more successfully preserved old-country norms). During the progressive era other institutions offered the same benefits, and more. Unions offered higher wages, job security, and accident insurance. Government seemed somewhat more responsive to immigrant needs, as evidenced by tenement laws, the construction of parks and playgrounds, limited provision for workmen's compensation and the eight-hour day, and exemption of labor unions from antitrust prosecution. Although still suspicious that progressives might use the government for cultural coercion (through Prohibition, compulsory public school attendance, immigration restriction) immigrants forged alliances with urban political machines,'' which John Buenker demonstrates (*Urban Liberalism and Progressive Reform,* 1973) were in the forefront of reform. Immigrants did not unthinkingly barter away their votes, nor did ''bosses'' unscrupulously manipulate their constituents for venal ends. Ironically, social and economic legislation may have accelerated acculturation more effectively than cultural coercion, by increasing mobility and contact with people outside of ethnic communities.

Ethnic institutions proliferated in the years before World War I, but their functions changed. Second generation Italians, argues Humbert Nelli (*The Italians in Chicago, 1880-1930,* 1970), showed little interest in the foreign language press; marriage with non-Italians became increasingly commonplace. Ignoring or underemphasizing civic or neighborhood activities, societies focused almost exclusively on Italian history and public affairs. Italians inaugurated the movement to make Columbus Day a national holiday. They gathered money for earthquake victims in Italy. Even appeals to Italian nationalism, however, did not always receive an enthusiastic response. A drive to collect money to present the city of Buffalo with a statue of Giuseppe Verdi languished for six years. The societies nonetheless survived—because they remained refuges from prejudice, places to reaffirm ethnic heritage symbolically without renouncing American values.

During the past decade historians and social commentators have praised the durability and usefulness of ethnic allegiances (Michael Novak, *The Rise of the Unmeltable Ethnics: Politics and Culture in the Seventies,* 1972). Such an analysis, John Higham suggests (*Send These Unto Me: Jews and Other Immigrants in Urban America,* 1975), does not adequately account for the complexities of immigrant life. Most immigrants joined ethnic organizations, although they desired to absorb American culture and did not view ''success'' as a measure of disloyalty to the group. Solidarity within each nationality, moreover, was not monolithic, nor were immigrants (who disagreed about religion, politics, and the family as vehemently as people born in America) a united, embattled enclave in conflict with an Anglo culture. Aware that adapting to American society was a necessity, they Americanized—sometimes enthusiastically, sometimes reluctantly. Yet as Milton Gordon points out, an end to associational life did not accompany the erosion of a distinctive culture. Acculturation without structural assimilation, achieved unevenly and not without stress and anxiety, enabled immigrants to gain security through group identity without diminishing economic mobility. Many immigrants, then, practiced a social theory before they consciously articulated it.

For immigrants who were socialists ethnic chauvinism was an acute problem because it impeded class solidarity. Ethnic and racial "myths," socialists believed, served capitalism by dividing working people. Old-World antagonisms, rekindled by proximity and job competition in the United States, sapped the strength of unions, in part because rank and file often opposed strikes not called by their nationality. Immigrant groups sometimes "scabbed" against one another—and few consented to alliances with blacks. Michael Gold's semi-autobiographical novel *Jews Without Money* (1930) centered on immigrant aspirations and the antagonism between Jewish and Irish families. In the process of organizing a rent strike, Mikey's mother finds that she has much in common with her Irish neighbors, but even so, suspicion on both sides prevents intimacy or a durable alliance. Ethnic pride and hostility, socialists believed, obscured the sources and realities of power and exploitation and diminished the possibility of international class coalitions.

Yet socialists were certainly unwilling to support Americanization which, they charged, was in the hands of the capitalists who used it to build a quiescent labor force. If ethnic nationalism was a problem, spread-eagle American patriotism could scarcely be a solution. Socialists charged that Americanization had been the club that menaced Haymarket radicals Alexander

Berkman (the anarchist who tried to assassinate industrialist Henry Clay Frick) and Johann Most, the fiery German exile. They knew that government officials had discredited socialism as an "alien idea," a policy formalized by the Alien Deportation Act of 1903, which gave Congress full power to exclude aliens if their views were "dangerous to the public welfare." The government grimly exercised its option against Emma Goldman and other "troublemakers." Americanization, then would continue to be an evil force as long as capitalists controlled it—and the government. World War I underscored this dilemma, as socialists tortured themselves in deciding whether to support American participation in the war. Americanization, some argued, churned out soldiers ready to die for imperialism. Ethnic insularity *and* American values, socialists concluded, had to be transcended to make a revolution, but in the meantime what was to be done?

A few socialists reluctantly decided to use ethnic allegiances to transcend ethnic parochialism. They counted on the environment to erode ethnicity in the long run, but to ignore it at present was to court failure. Consequently immigrants made socialist appeals in foreign language newspapers like *Il Progresso* and *The Forward*. Even socialist organizations and unions recruited along ethnic lines. During the textile strike of 1912 in Lawrence, Massachusetts—a mill town with immigrants representing fifty-one countries—the Industrial Workers of the World succeeded in forming a Strike Committee that represented all ethnic groups (Melvyn Dubofsky, *We Shall Be All: A History of the I.W.W.,* 1969). Class solidarity was the message, issued in scores of languages, but socialists recognized the fragility of the coalitions they forged.

Although substantial numbers of immigrants were attracted to socialism, a belief that socialists sought cultural homogenization persisted. Immigrants did not share the view that the issue of restriction should be cast in terms of what was best for labor as a whole, nor did they necessarily accept the Marxist assertion that the machine and industrial rhythms were a phase of history that would ultimately lead to equality and abundance. Often attracted to the economic critique of the socialists, most immigrants resisted subordinating ethnicity to the class struggle.

A concern that corporate power choked individual opportunity and bred frustration and anger among workers motivated the progressive reforms of the early twentieth century (Peter Filene doubts that a progressive *movement* existed: "An Obituary for Progressivism," 1970). Concentrated in urban ghettoes, immigrants presented the most visible evidence of industrial exploitation and constituted, progressives agreed, a palpable threat to social order. The prosperity of the new century afforded an excellent opportunity to make American society more humane and democratic without endangering economic and political institutions. In this sense progressives were reformist conservatives who acted confidently to regulate the excesses of industrialism while providing equality of opportunity to the foreigners in their midst.

Many progressives asserted that because the environment was the main factor in shaping personality, American society had an obligation to help provide a more wholesome environment for citizens of all "races." (Few in this era distinguished between racial and ethnic group.) They were far more confident of achieving this goal for European "races" than for blacks and Orientals even though their source authority, Franz Boas, made no such distinctions in his rejection of hereditary determinism and fixed racial types. Dismissing as unscientific assertions that immigrants could not adapt to the American environment, the anthropologist found that:

the head form, which has always been considered one of the most stable and permanent characteristics of human races, undergoes far-reaching changes due to the transfer of the people from European to American soil. . . . This fact shows. . .that not even those characteristics of a race which have proved to be most permanent in their old home remain the same under the new surroundings; and we are compelled to conclude that when these features of the body change, the whole bodily and mental make-up of the immigrant may change. . . . All the evidence is now in favor of a great plasticity of human types.

Although few completely embraced Boas' sweeping conclusions, settlement workers, the vanguard of progressivism in ethnicity even more than they had been in race, insisted that the stunted growth of immigrants resulted primarily from stultifying living conditions (Allen F. Davis, *Spearheads For Reform,* 1967). "Until industrial conditions in America are faced," Jane Addams, the founder of Hull House in Chicago, asserted, "the immigrant will continue to be blamed for conditions for which the community is responsible." Settlement workers lived among the immigrants with the dual purpose of lifting the most capable out of the ghetto and improving the lot of those who remained.

Intent upon the moral and aesthetic purification of immigrant life, the settlement workers promoted parks, libraries, and cleaner streets. Schools reopened at night as theatres, assembly halls, and municipal baths. Art exhibits featuring the paintings of neighborhood people were sponsored. The settlement house, however, was not merely, as one critic would have it, a cultural "comfort station...upholding a standard of tight-smiling prissiness." Settlement workers were eminently practical: they provided classes for immigrant women in cooking, sewing, and shopping; they demonstrated support of unions in meetings and on picket lines: they coaxed public schools to adopt vocational guidance, school nurses, and school lunches. Convinced that a rural environment fostered virtue (Jean Quandt, *From the Small Town to the Great Community,* 1970), they set up summer camps for immigrant youths and sought to reopen the frontier by relocating ghetto dwellers in the farming hinterlands. The reformers believed that their principal task was to help immigrants lift themselves from poverty to the middle class. Settlements, asserted Jacob Riis, whose photographs indelibly imprinted the degradations of ghetto life on the American consciousness (*How the Other Half Lives,* 1890), provided bridges out of the ghetto. While charity did not help immigrants help themselves, education and voluntary efforts to reconstruct the environment provided ambition and skills, the prerequisites for success in America.

Very quickly, however, settlement workers concluded that their voluntary efforts were not sufficient to break the cycle of poverty, and turned to the government for help. Although they shared the concern of their contemporaries that legislation sometimes threatened individual initiative, these progressives insisted that government must regulate those excesses of capitalism that destroyed opportunity, thereby diminishing liberty. The New York Tenement Law of 1901 is an example of the reformers' view of constructive legislation. The law, which did not commit the government to housing construction, forced landlords to provide adequate ventilation, fire protection, and toilet facilities in every building and set up a Tenement House Department to investigate violations. The freedom to construct buildings of any design had to be balanced against the duty of the state to protect the health and welfare of its citizens. Action at the local and state level, moreover, was deemed insufficient by many progressives whose agitation produced a National Child Labor Act, Pure Food and Drug Act, Workmen's Compensation Act, and exemption of unions from antitrust legislation. To the settlement workers—men and women infused with Protestant morality and noblesse oblige—free enterprise must not be accompanied by ethical laissez-faire nor official indifference to the conditions that produced poverty; economic regulation was sometimes moral legislation.

If reaction to life in the ghetto spurred progressive reform, the programs of settlement workers nonetheless sometimes aroused the resentment of immigrants. Immigrant men, irked at the daily doses of culture administered to their wives during the day were angered when reformers encouraged women to handle family resources. Although immigrants agreed about the importance of educating their children, they often found it necessary to ignore child labor laws because the meager pay brought home by children often meant the difference between subsistence and starvation. Finally, the suggestion by a few settlement workers that immigration restriction would reduce the labor pool, and thereby increase wages and improve working conditions, infuriated immigrants, who often had parents, spouses, and children in the Old World. The settlement workers, many believed, were in the ghetto but not of it. So intent on helping immigrants reach the promised land of the middle class, so certain that they had objectively discerned the best interests of the newcomers, the reformers sometimes spoke before they listened and called for sacrifices that immigrants were not inclined to make.

In recent years a few historians have condemned settlement workers for forcing the immigrants to jettison Old-World customs in favor of an antiseptic middle-class model, and for optimistically proposing to help the disadvantaged out of the ghetto without disturbing democratic capitalism, social equilibrium, or the Protestant ethic. While it may well be that the reformers were naive in thinking that economic and political equality of opportunity could be extended to all without fundamental alterations in American institutions, their achievements should not be minimized nor their motives impugned. Because they believed that environment shaped character and that the distinguishing characteristic of human beings was their capacity to plan rationally, the settlement workers insisted that government could and should act to remove impediments to equality of opportunity. Nonetheless, in contrast even to some of their fellow progressives (Roger Daniels, *The Politics of Prejudice,* 1962), most settlement workers did not think that cultural coercion was a legitimate function of government. With John Dewey they believed that only if a society transmitted its knowledge and values to newcomers, could succeeding generations build and improve on the past. Effective cultural transmission, however, had to be voluntary. A fundamental alteration in social thought was beginning to emerge. Most nineteenth-century reformers accepted economic laissez-faire and moral and cultural legislation as articles of faith. Now, more and more progressives sanctioned some economic regulation, and a few called for increased tolerance of cultural differences.

The reformers, then, transmitted their values to immigrants because they were certain that they provided a passage out of poverty and into the good life. Many settlement workers, moreover, had a healthier respect for immigrant traditions than the vast majority of their contemporaries. Jane Addams constantly advised immigrants to "preserve and keep whatever of value their past life contained," although she realized that some traditions and norms of behavior (could Jews refuse to work on their Sabbath in Protestant America?) had to be undermined. The socialization of immigrants, as noted, seems particularly objectionable because, unlike children, they are not cultural *tabulae rasae*. But socialization there must be. Armed with what they perceived as superior values, admirably suited to an industrial age, yet infused with Protestant morality and aesthetic appreciation, the settlement workers, not surprisingly, did not shrink from cajoling, persuading, and at times badgering immigrants to discard their "inferior" cultural baggage.

In the first decades of the twentieth century, pressure for Americanization mounted. Earlier, industrialists had been ambivalent about Americanization because they believed (as did many socialists) that ethnic hostilities constituted a barrier against union solidarity. Employers slowly became convinced, however, that unions could be checked in other ways, while Americanization could increase factory productivity. Progressives indirectly forced the issue by passing legislation mandating safe conditions and requiring companies to compensate injured workers and their families. No longer did laborers have to prove company negligence in order to collect. With this new incentive to insure safety, industrial firms employed interpreters to explain factory regulations and cooperated with state agencies to develop movies which taught safety in a "universal tongue." Industrialists recognized, however, that teaching English to immigrants was the best insurance against costly accidents.

As they recognized that Americanization improved the performance of immigrants on the job, corporate managers pounced upon English language programs, developed in many instances by progressives (Gerd Korman, *Industrialization, Immigrants, and Americanizers,* 1967). Many companies adopted Peter Roberts' YMCA program because it taught English for three spheres of life: domestic, industrial, and commercial. Immigrants learned how to dress, tip, buy groceries, and vote. The program designed for International Harvester reveals how language instruction served the needs of industrialists:

> I hear the whistle. I must hurry.
> I hear the five minute whistle.
> It is time to go into the shop.
> I take my check from the gate board and hang it
>   on the department board.
> I change my clothes and get ready to work.
> The starting whistle blows.
> I eat my lunch.
> It is forbidden to eat until then.
> The whistle blows at five minutes of starting time.
> I get ready to go to work.
> I work until the whistle blows to quit.
> I leave my place nice and clean.
> I put all my clothes in my locker.
> I go home.

Learning the language, then, meant acclimating oneself to the industrial cycle. Advanced lessons taught immigrants the benevolence of their employers. Boss Brown of U.S. Steel "treats his men right, and he expects his men to treat him right." An integral part of industrial paternalism, Americanization—supplemented by lunchrooms, employee lounges, recreation clubs, and opera companies—defused discontent and presumably undermined the appeal of unions. Sophisticated employers were willing to spend a few dollars if productivity increased and workers identified with their benevolent bosses.

The antiforeign feeling unleashed by World War I strengthened the tendency of many progressives to support Americanization even if programs destroyed ethnic culture. To an extent attention shifted from southern and eastern Europeans to German-Americans, who before the war had often been compared favorably with the "new immigrants." Many reformers now agreed that the imperative of national unity justified a government-sanctioned suppression of all things German. As the Creel Committee on Public Information whipped up anti-German sentiment, Congress gave the Postmaster General virtually absolute power over foreign language newspapers, while granting the executive *carte blanche* to punish opinions "disloyal, profane, scurrilous or abusive to the American form of government, flag or uniform." Many state legislatures banned German from the public school curriculum, scores of towns and cities changed their names to remove any teutonic taint, German music disappeared from concert halls, and sauerkraut became "liberty cabbage." The old racist arguments, once reserved for "new immigrants" were refashioned to fit Germans. Madison Grant reissued his race-suicide tract, *The Passing of the Great Race,* in 1918, shorn of all references to German contributions to American civilization, while other works claimed that Germans were actually descended from Asian barbarians. Former President Roosevelt advocated death to German-American spies and by implication to an autonomous German-American culture: "He who is not with us, absolutely and without reserve of any kind, is against us, and should be treated as an alien enemy. Our bitter experience should teach us for a generation...to crush under our heel every movement that smacks in the smallest degree of playing the German game." German immigrants were sometimes dragged into the streets and forced to kiss the flag. The conviction of a man for speaking German to his parrot epitomized the terrible absurdities of war hysteria. The conversion of Americans from neutrality to virulent partnership was accomplished by depicting the Huns as rabid beasts—and President Wilson ruefully acknowledged the government's role in sacrificing toleration at home to the exigencies of unity and mobilization.

Although the German-Americans were the chief targets of overt violence, most immigrant groups suffered from what John Higham has called "the anti-hyphenate animus." The National Americanization Committee summed up a prevalent attitude: "Let us insist frankly that a man born on another soil has to prove himself for America." Such sentiments issued in statutes in Utah and Idaho that required aliens to attend classes in Americanization and in the draconian Sedition Act of 1918, under which 6,300 enemy aliens were arrested. The Farmer's National Congress suggested that these undesirables be branded prior to deportation to prevent their return. Although the foreign-born constituted 18 percent of the U.S. Army, more than their proportion of the total population, xenophobia often prevailed.

"One-hundred-percent Americans" turned to industrial Americanization programs as the best way to instill patriotism in the foreigners. In this effort they supported Frances Kellor, a settlement worker turned Rooseveltian New Nationalist, who for years had urged her fellow progressives to make "a conscious effort to forge the people of this country into an American race that will stand together for America in time of peace and war." With the declaration of war, she renewed her call by contrasting the ominous scene of radical agitators haranguing immigrants in their own language with the first English words of a new citizen: "I am an American."

Industrial managers, delighted at this outpouring of support for Americanization programs, bent them to their own purposes. As the war slowed immigration to a trickle, new influxes of competing workers could no longer be used to keep immigrants at the workplaces. Industrialists put immigrants, radicals, and other agitators on the defensive by branding strikers "traitors" or "soviets" and contrasting their efforts to promote national unity through Americanization programs with the disruption of the economy by unions. The "melting pot has not melted," declared the educational director of the National Security League. League President Charles B. Leydecker worried about "dangerous proletarians," whom he defined as members of society who are "devoid of thrift, industry, or any accumulation by reason therefore. . . . Our imported people are, unfortunately, some of them of that class." In such an atmosphere it is not surprising that the radical union, the I.W.W., suffered from the harassment and deportation of its foreign-born members. Patriotism, many industrialists discovered, enhanced production and profits.

Once unleashed, xenophobia could not easily be turned off when the war ended. Immigrants still served as convenient targets, responsible for all disruptions of "normalcy." Woodrow Wilson blamed them for the defeat of the Versailles Treaty that ended World War I and created the League of Nations: "Hyphens are the knives that are being stuck in this document." Attorney General A. Mitchell Palmer capitalized on anti-immigrant prejudice by raiding nests of "communist insurgents," deporting, often without trial, aliens whom he thought a danger to the social fabric. Palmer, as Robert K. Murray has shown (*Red Scare, A Study in National Hysteria, 1919–1920,* 1955), cried wolf too often to satisfy his presidential ambitions, but antiforeign feeling did not diminish when he was discredited. Henry Ford's interest in the Bolshevist Protocols of Zion, and the trial of Sacco and Vanzetti, are only two celebrated instances of xenophobia in the 1920s. The resurrected Ku Klux Klan, moreover, was not merely a rural Southern movement intent on refighting the Civil War (Kenneth Jackson, *The Ku Klux Klan in the City, 1915–1930,* 1967). The Klan, which limited membership to native-born Protestants, drew much of its membership from cities buffeted by sizable immigrant populations. Klan programs called for compulsory education, the interdiction of land ownership by aliens, an end to the "Columbus Legend" and the proper recognition of Leif Erickson. In Portland, Oregon, the Kluxers "escorted" I.W.W. members out of the city. The strength of the Klan apparently lay in its ability to define the organization as an effective agent of Americanization.

Five years after the defeat of the Versailles treaty, Congress passed the first comprehensive immigration restriction bill in the nation's history. Pseudo-scientific racism, postwar xenophobia and diminished faith in the capacity of American institutions to absorb a new flood of immigrants convinced legislators that restriction must be enacted immediately. Qualms about government control over the flow of immigration had evidently disappeared, even amid the laissez-faire rhetoric of Coolidge and Harding, as the bill passed the House by a vote of 276 to 33 and the Senate with only one dissenting vote. Representative Tincher of Kansas articulated the prevailing view: "On the one side is beer, bolshevism, unassimilating settlements and perhaps many flags—on the other side is constitutional government; one flag, stars and stripes." Although racists like Madison Grant and Lathrop Stoddard supported restriction, they embarrassed many of the bill's supporters who viewed immigration in political and economic terms—and in some instances rejected the notion that immigrants were biologically inferior. The legislation won the support of businessmen and labor leaders, who knew that the return of American troops from Europe necessitated the integration of a large pool of workers into a scaled-down, peacetime economy. Fearful that demobilization might be accompanied by depression, labor leaders did not want the added complication of job competition by a new wave of immigrants. Cloaked in 100 percent Americanism, Samuel Gompers supported restriction. Now that the labor pool was large enough to insure management a substantial advantage over the unions, especially given technological advances that replaced workers with machines, businessmen also saw little benefit in massive immigration. Outside of the immigrants themselves, few organized groups defended America as asylum.

The restriction legislation passed by Congress in 1921 and 1924 was directed against southern and eastern Europeans, labelled in one report as "filthy, un-American and often dangerous in their habits." Through a complicated legislative formula, Congress ultimately limited immigration to 2 percent of the number of foreign-born residents of each nationality who lived in the United States in 1890. Since most of the new immigrants came after 1890, the legislation clearly discriminated against them. The acts also continued the traditional exclusion of Asiatics. To some extent, restriction revealed diminished faith in, but not repudiation of, Americanization. In the disillusionment that followed the war, most Americans doubted that their institutions could absorb unlimited numbers of immigrants. Amid the flight from responsibility that characterized much of the 1920s' "Jazz Age," many Americans were willing to "solve" the perplexing problems of ethnic diversity by drastically reducing the number of immigrant men and women to be educated, housed, and provided with economic opportunity.

If World War I stimulated coercive Americanization programs, it also prompted several intellectuals to reexamine ethnicity and the role of the State in fostering cultural diversity. Significantly, Horace Kallen and Randolph Bourne, the first self-proclaimed "cultural pluralists," were students of the pragmatic philosophy of William James and John Dewey. Pragmatism, in Morton White's apt phrase (*Social Thought in America: The Revolt Against Formalism,* 1949), was a "revolt against formalism." Pragmatists denied that they were utilitarians, but they did argue for the "validity" of an approach if it "worked" for its practitioner. William James dealt sympathetically with many "varieties of religious experience"; each deserved praise for the comfort it brought or the action it spurred. Pragmatists argued that because time, place, and people inevitably shifted contexts, no single law could govern society or political economy. Effective freedom, and therefore progress, were not possible without a milieu that encouraged a variety of answers and approaches. Pragmatism was impossible without pluralism.

Jamesean pluralism focused on individuals; Dewey concerned himself with the interaction between the individual and society; Bourne and Kallen applied pluralism to the coexistence of cultures within a nation-state. Both men praised the settlement workers and endorsed progressive efforts to regulate the economy and ameliorate conditions in the ghetto. In fact, they believed that government had not gone far enough in guaranteeing genuine equality of opportunity. Nonetheless they also sought to articulate a social theory that committed government to cultural laissez-faire by enumerating the benefits of "toleration." Kallen, a native Silesian, Harvard-educated Zionist, implied that ethnic characteristics were immutable in essays that set forth the value of ethnic pluralism: "An Irishman is always an Irishman, a Jew always a Jew. Irishman or Jew is born; citizen, lawyer, or church member is made." In a series of articles in *The Nation* (1915) entitled "Democracy Versus the Melting Pot," Kallen asserted that the Constitutional guarantee of federalism should be applicable to national cultures. If individuals remained free to choose a religion or political party, groups must be free to preserve their ethnic heritage. The availability of such options, Kallen argued—clearly echoing James and Dewey—was the *sine qua non* of democracy: "The political and economic life of the commonwealth is a single unit and serves as the foundation and background for the realization of the distinctive individuality of each *natio* that composes it and of the pooling of these in a common harmony above them all. Thus 'American Civilization' may come to mean the perfection of the cooperative harmonies of 'European civilization'—the waste, the squalor and the distress of Europe being eliminated—a multiplicity in a unity, an orchestration of mankind." Unlike the genteel class, Kallen celebrated the Europeanization of the United States, because he believed that a healthy, vigorous nation would emerge from the interplay of cultures. If the frontier no longer provided a guarantee of democracy, a variety of nationalities, in the very acts of competition and toleration, guarded freedom. Ethnic diversity, then, was the new foundation of Madisonian pluralism.

Kallen's rejection of the melting pot was a reaction to Americanization programs that evinced contempt or condescension for ethnic culture. Such Anglo-Saxon chauvinism William James had long since denounced as "sniveling cant." Concerned that the equation of Anglo-Saxon and American cultures was dangerous, Kallen nonetheless defiantly proclaimed that although Americanization might force small changes in outward behavior, it could not transform the "inner man." Collective identity was an indomitable characteristic of human society: "Democracy involves not the elimination of differences but the perfection and conservation of differences." All United States citizens spoke a common language, but each person retained the freedom to carve out spheres of influence for his or her ancestral culture.

Kallen's theory of cultural pluralism, though undeniably attractive in comparison to antihyphenate Americanization programs, was vague as a guide to social action. At times cultural pluralism purported to describe existing conditions; at times it prescribed the ideal in group relationships. If ethnic identity was as immutable as Kallen asserted it to be, Americanization posed little danger. Nor was Kallen clear on what government could do to promote cultural pluralism. Would education, economic opportunity, and ghetto improvement in fact erode a distinctive immigrant culture? Upton Sinclair, Abraham Cahan, and others admitted that inner changes occurred when immigrants altered their external behavior. The workplace and the schoolhouse were effective instruments of socialization; foreign language newspapers constantly lamented that the second generation ignored its heritage. Immigrants were probably less resistant to cultural erosion than Kallen thought or desired them to be.

Like virtually all of his contemporaries (Du Bois' stress on African culture is, of course, a notable exception), Kallen viewed American civilization as a harmony of European civilizations. Thus, as John Higham has pointed out, Kallen's cultural pluralism, like that of so many progressives, was "encapsulated in white ethnocentrism." In essence, he emerged with a thesis that traced culture to ethnic and national origins, ignored class, and downplayed the necessity of sacrificing traditions to economic imperatives. Kallen's achievement nonetheless was remarkable: in the midst of virulent prejudice against immigrants and often unthinking reverence for the melting pot, he posed an alternative which preserved the integrity of the group, enhanced the opportunities of individuals, and enriched the nation.

Impressed with Kallen's theory, Randolph Bourne believed that cultural pluralism provided an answer to the frightening tendencies of war fever. A student of John Dewey and Franz Boaz at Columbia University, Bourne embraced the progressive tendency to snatch "at one after the other idea, programme, movement, ideal, to uplift them out of the slough in which they slept...by reviving the Ten Comandments for political purposes." Bourne's dissatisfaction came not with too much government regulation but with the coalition of the propertied class and the State. During World War I these apprehensions issued in a warning that the State, in its insatiable voraciousness, demanded individual sacrifice, an end to dissent, and an assault on group loyalties, in the name of patriotism and national survival. The war, then, reminded Bourne of the fragility of pluralism and the free marketplace of ideas, and of the tendency of the State to demand loyalty rather than enhance freedom.

Although an Anglo-Saxon, Bourne's physical deformity (he was a hunchback) enhanced his sympathy for "outsiders." In the 1916 essay "Trans-National America," he asserted that cultural pluralism, "a higher ideal than the melting pot," was the best bulwark against the State, as well as the nation's only insurance against stagnation. Group security fostered by tenacious cultural allegiance provided a significant check on the State's siren call to loyalty. Pluralists did not want an America that "is interested only for economic exploitation of the workers or for predatory economic imperialism among the weaker peoples. They do not want one that is integrated by coercion or militarism, or for the truculent assertion of a medieval code of honor and of doubtful rights. They believe that the most effective integration will be one which coordinates the diverse elements and turns them consciously toward working out together the place of America in the world situation." Bourne, like Kallen, took federalism seriously. He envisioned an American "world federation in miniature," a heterogeneous people gaining strength from the acceptance of difference. Dual citizenship was a higher form of patriotism.

Although Bourne, like Kallen, celebrated the persistence of ethnic culture, he recognized that cultural pluralism was not the reigning dogma in the United States nor even the credo of most progressives. If freedom meant "a democratic cooperation in determining the ideals and purposes and industrial and social institutions of a country," then immigrants remained unfree. Cultural pluralism, he believed, would help wrest the control of government from the wealthy, who used Americanization to promote stability and conformity; yet because cultural pluralism provided a defense against economic exploitation, instituting it as a goal of social policy would be most difficult. Bourne's essay ended with a call to action rather than a program of action: "Let us face realistically the America we have around us. Let us work with the forces that are at work. Let us make something of this transnational spirit instead of outlawing it. . . . What we need everywhere is a vivid consciousness of the new ideal. . . . To make this striving among dangers and apathies is work for a younger intelligentsia of America." Bourne died in 1918, a victim of the flu epidemic, before he could develop a program capable of overcoming the power of Americanizers.

The proponents of pluralism, reacting primarily to the strident Americanization of World War I, spoke to the future rather than their present when they insisted that heterogeneity was a positive rather than disruptive force. Their debate with Americanizers, however, indicated that a dramatic shift had taken place in ethnic thought within the short span of a generation. Whether immigrants *should* Americanize, rather than whether they *could,* was now the central question. Both sides accepted an expanded role for the government in guaranteeing freedom and equality, though they had grave differences on the nature of that role. The 1920s "return to normalcy" was in reality a brief interlude that should not obscure the kinship of progressives, pluralists, the New Deal "broker state," and the recent ethnic renaissance.

THREE

Coming to Terms with Class Differences

Industrialism altered the American social landscape. Large-scale production spurred immigration and swelled cities, providing laborers and consumers who fueled production. This cycle changed the lives of Americans and, as we have seen, changed the ways in which they thought about their lives. In the industrial Gilded Age, as Robert Bremner has shown (*From the*

Depths: The Discovery of Poverty in the U.S., 1956), poverty was "discovered." There had always been poor people in America, of course, but now it seemed that unskilled factory laborers constituted a permanent working class, trapped in urban ghettoes. Dramatic contrasts between pauperism and plenty, between plutocrats and workers, between the circle of the Social Register and the cycle of poverty, became the "stuff" of novels, paintings, and journalistic jeremiads, which hinted darkly about cataclysmic social conflict.

Events like the Haymarket Riot, the Pullman Strike, and the march of Coxey's Army lent credence to fears of industrial warfare. Native-born workers, "drifting and sliding to nowhere," immigrant "strangers in a strange land," made ideal recruits for revolution, who might in concert bring Europe to America—the Europe of poverty and Paris communes. The impending crisis, some believed, might take the form of a "class conflict" between the producers and the speculative parasites. Few Americans, to be sure, conceived of "class" in Marxist terms although most, either implicitly or explicitly, linked human behavior to economic imperatives. A turn-of-the-century dictionary lists generally accepted characteristics of class: "equality in rank, intellectual influence, education, property, occupation, habits of life." Americans often added a moral component to this definition: the prosperous were virtuous and industrious, the poor vicious and indolent. Class conflict, a term used more widely in the twentieth century than in the nineteenth, usually referred to a struggle between the rich and the poor, the powerful and the powerless, the capitalists and the workers, the plutocrats and the masses. These categories were seldom defined with precision, but vagueness scarcely dispelled the spectre of a bloody uprising of the lower classes.

Although most Americans agreed that provision for equality of opportunity provided the best protection against industrial conflict, sharp differences about how to guarantee such equality characeized social thought in the late nineteenth century. Taking the Darwinian doctrine of "survival of the fittest" as axiomatic, some maintained that competition, unhindered by government or misguided "do-gooders," facilitated economic mobility without handicapping those of superior ability. Others, no less influenced by Darwin, argued that cooperation had replaced competition in the evolutionary scheme, rendering laissez-faire as extinct as *tyrannosauras rex.* Rational planning, at times implemented by institutions of government, must be the keynote of social policy. By the end of the century the Populists, as indicated in Chapter One, insisted that government regulate the economy in the name of the "producing classes." Populism was mortally wounded in the election of 1896 but the program of the People's party was adopted, almost *in toto,* by 1920.

The prosperity of the early twentieth century did not erase the memory of industrial strife nor eliminate the fear of class conflict. An essay in the school newspaper of St. Mark's Missionary Society is a case in point:

The majority of the boys in this school are the sons of wealthy or well-to-do parents, at any event they are members of the so-called 'upper classes'. . . . Very few of us will be forced to the misnamed degradation of manual labor, and will consider ourselves superior to and will hold positions of authority over the laboring classes. We are evidently on the verge of another social upheaval [which]. . .may even break out into the horrors of an inter-class war. . . . How much better it will be for us to learn to understand the other class now!

Understanding "the other class," progressive reformers insisted, must be accompanied by laws and practices that encouraged and protected the interest-group organizations of the lower classes, while outlawing the unethical and monopolistic practices of corporations. During the progressive era, James Weinstein has argued (*The Corporate Ideal in the Liberal State, 1900–1918,* 1968), laissez-faire gave way to "an ideal of responsible social order in which all classes could look forward to some form of recognition and sharing in the benefits of an ever-expanding economy." Government and loyalty to the national interest, however, must stand above all classes so that self-interest did not give way to selfishness. Classes would always exist because differences in occupation, status, and wealth were as "natural" as they were inevitable, yet progressives remained firmly convinced that a reformed and regulated capitalism, by providing abundance, mobility, and opportunity to all, made class conflict literally and figuratively unproductive.

Throughout much of their history Americans boasted that the nation, in contrast to Europe, was relatively free of fixed categories of social class. Echoing the brilliant nineteenth-century political philosopher Alexis de Tocqueville, Louis Hartz (*The Liberal Tradition in America,* 1955) attributes American uniqueness to the fact that the people were "born free," without feudal institutions, and therefore without a system of permanent distinctions, responsibilities, and rights between serf and master. In America an individual's clothing and speech did not accurately reveal status or occupation, nor did a titled aristocracy or a court entourage preempt political power. Patterns of deference existed, to be sure, but depended upon custom and not law—slavery of course is the notorious exception—and keen observers like de Tocqueville and James Fenimore Cooper noted that custom was often ignored. By the time of the American Revolution few even dared to call themselves "Esquire" or "Gent," and those, like John Adams, who sought to reserve a branch of the legislature for each social class, were dismissed as monarchists. The nation's royal family was to be all the people, undifferentiated by formal social rank.

In practice of course, status distinctions existed, but in America social class depended far more upon wealth than birth. One can (and many did) exaggerate the amount of geographic and economic mobility, but relative to Europe, the United States *was* the land of opportunity. Abundant resources and land, laws prohibiting primogeniture and entail and the protection of continental isolation provided reasons for aspiration and expectation. Rags to riches were very rare but possible; poverty to middle-class comfort occurred frequently. The adages of Benjamin Franklin seemed rooted in reality, even for the poor. All could legitimately aspire to the status conferred by wealth. Therefore failure was often attributed to character defects: lack of industry, honesty, sobriety. In this fluid society, where money talked and pedigree failed to impress, classes certainly formed and even hardened, but Americans were more free and equal, and less inclined to think that they would die in the same social class to which they had been born.

America's religious, ethnic, and racial heterogeneity, as well as its relative social and economic fluidity, discouraged conflict between the "wealthy classes" and the "laboring classes." Well before the "new immigration" observers were struck by the diversity of the nation. In the last two decades social historians, influenced by the pioneering work of Lee Benson (*The Concept of Jacksonian Democracy,* 1961), have demonstrated the centrality of ethnocultural conflict in American life. Economic issues usually did not divide citizens with the intensity of conflicts over parochial schools and temperance. The intellectual baggage that English and Irish, Protestant and Catholic, black and white carried across the Atlantic included age-old hatreds, to be worn defiantly in the New World. In the United States the journey from poverty to prosperity—like the trek across the ocean—was desirable, difficult, but doable; often united in the scramble for wealth, Americans remained divided by race, religion, and ethnicity.

A commonplace of American social thought was that as long as free land, abundant resources, and a democratic government nourished expectations and rewarded effort, the nation would remain free from the conflict that ravaged Europe. The Louisiana Purchase and the Mexican Cession, many believed, were insurance policies that guaranteed farms for generations of middle-class yeomen. By the 1870s, however, industrialism presented the prospect of unbridgeable distances between wealth and poverty, and the possibility of violence by the frustrated urban masses.

As the United States "trembled between two worlds"—one rural and agricultural, the other urban and industrial—middle-class reformers at first applied traditional remedies to the nation's social ills: Protestant moral exhortation, voluntarism, and appeals to rural individualism. Although still attributing poverty to individual character defects, they worried that the industrial city separated the rich and poor, thereby robbing the latter of uplifting moral influences. The gap between the wealthy classes and the urban poor must be narrowed, but not through the indiscriminate dispensation of charity. If poverty was an outward badge of a weak character, insisted Josephine Shaw Lowell, director of the New York Charity Organization Society, then alms merely subsidized the indolent impulses of workers, without effecting their moral reformation. Much more preferable were visits to working class homes where reformers could investigate, exhort, and then dispense appropriate aid. To this end a host of organizations (the YMCA, the Home Missionary Society), some secular, some sectarian, often financed by merchants, manufacturers, and bankers, formed to reestablish ties between the classes. Once workers learned that effort insured success, their animus toward the wealthy classes might be replaced by deference and gratitude. Mrs. Lowell acknowledged that a mixture of altruism and self-interest governed the charity movement: a reform organization should "refuse to support any except those whom it can control."

Although the reformers attributed poverty to defects of character, they recognized that ghetto residence rendered regeneration difficult. Lowell, Charles Loring Brace, Robert Hartley, and others fondly remembered spending their youths in small communities where networks of social obligations fostered moral development. The city, by contrast, provided no end of temptations for the weak: saloons, brothels, gambling houses. The moral reformers, despite some surface optimism, were not sanguine that miracles could be worked in such iniquitous surroundings, and sought to relocate the poor in the rural hinterland. Brace's Children's Aid Society placed street urchins with families in the West to be "absorbed into that active, busy population." As Paul Boyer has shrewdly observed (*Urban Masses and Moral Order,* 1978), Brace's continued belief in "self-help" resulted in a professed lack of interest in the success or failure of the transplanted adolescents. The Society had given "their ambition. . .scope for exercise''; whether or not they took advantage of the opportunity was their own affair. A potential mass of flammable material, in any event, would be scattered over the continent. The impact of the Society's efforts, however, was negligible; thousands moved to the interior, but tens of thousands took their places in the cities. The reformers baled water with a thimble and a large bucket of nostalgia: rural virtue could not be brought to the urban masses.

Deeply ingrained patterns of thought do not disappear quickly, even when they no longer reflect social reality. Thus the language of individual responsibility and rural virtue remained potent in the late nineteenth century. The popular novels of Horatio Alger celebrated hard work and sobriety by contrasting the "good fortune" of Ragged Dick and Mark the Matchboy with the fate of their dissolute friends. Alger, Richard Weiss has pointed out ("Horatio Alger Jr. and the Response to Industrialism," 1968), spent his youth in agricultural Marlborough, Massachusetts. His books appealed to people who abhorred the industrial city and wished to accept change without undermining values associated with the rural past. Neither immigrants, corporations, nor robber barons clutter Alger's streets. The honest and energetic heroes earn the rewards of Providence in the form of a chance to win the gratitude of a well-to-do merchant. Alger, and the scores of writers who used the genre, asserted that success, defined as middle-class respectability, awaited those who could summon the will to grasp it; yet lurking not far from the surface is the disquieting suspicion that the virtues of industry, piety, and sobriety were anachronistic platitudes in a world where kindly benefactors had been replaced by faceless corporations.

As the redeeming power of rural virtue began to lose its credibility, a new philosophy of individualism rose to take its place. The Englishman Herbert Spencer sought to apply Darwinist evolutionary theory to human development. Indeed, Spencer, not Darwin, coined the term "survival of the fittest." Spencer's theory of social selection (his philosophical and sociological works sold remarkably well in the United States) postulated the inevitability and asserted the desirability of economic and social stratification. Inequality was natural; the human species could improve only if the fittest survived and the weaklings perished. For the good of humankind this "natural order" must not be disturbed. Government-supported poor laws, education, tariffs, and sanitation merely penalized the superior in favor of the inferior. Charity, which produced dregs who could only burden future generations, was simply not rational.

The foremost American disciple of Spencer was Yale Professor William Graham Sumner. Wealthy people, Sumner believed, were frugal, sober, and industrious people who deserved success just as the poor merited their misery. Like Spencer, Sumner feared that government intervention in the economy would upset natural selection. Laissez-faire insured unrestricted competition, protected equality of opportunity (by providing a fair field with no favors), and guaranteed the survival of the fittest. Unlike Spencer, Sumner supported public education, but this was the only exception to a determinism that located ability in biology and scoffed at the capacity of the environment to improve people. Stateways, he wrote, probably could not and certainly should not change folkways. Sumner's answer to the question *What Social Classes Owe to Each Other* (1883) was: not much. Nature, he claimed, prescribes such an indifferent course:

If we do not like it, and if we try to amend it, there is only one way in which we can do it. We can take from the better and give to the worse. We can deflect the penalties of those who have done ill and throw them on those who have done better. . . . We shall thus lessen the inequalities. . . and we shall accomplish this by destroying liberty. Let it be understood that we cannot get outside this alternative: liberty, inequality, survival of the fittest; non-liberty, equality, survival of the unfittest.

Evolution disproved the validity of doctrines of equality; individuals must look to themselves and not others if they really wanted to succeed.

These Social Darwinist ideas, argued Richard Hofstadter (*Social Darwinism in American Thought,* 1944), had great appeal for businessmen because they justified their success and methods. Andrew Carnegie and Spencer, for example, became close friends. More recently, historians have reassessed the impact of Social Darwinism on American thought. The apparent moral neutrality of Social Darwinism flew in the face of Christian and community ideals. Horatio Alger's novels, where God, and merchants with beautiful daughters, *did* help those who helped themselves, certainly urged an active social commitment upon readers. The motive force behind the charity work of Lowell and Brace was that social classes *did* owe one another something. Just as importantly, Social Darwinism was in essence a negativist doctrine that seemed to advise the "fittest" to sit idly by as industrialism, urban overcrowding, strikes, and crime threatened social order. Assurances that misery and poverty were "natural," many realized, were not likely to give pause to starving workers who refused to die to improve the species. Social Darwinsim had a limited audience in the United States, then, because it offered no realistic program to establish social stability to people increasingly convinced that the "natural" course of events might well be anarchy or revolution.

And the fear of class conflict was everywhere. Cataclysmic thought, Frederic Jaher has demonstrated (*Doubters and Dissenters: Cataclysmic Thought in America, 1885-1918,* 1964), characterized much of the literature of the era. Brooks Adams' *Law of Civilization and Decay* (1893), Mary E. Lease's *The Problem of Civilization Solved* (1895), and Jack London's *The Iron Heel* (1906) shared a morbid fascination with an impending uprising of the "lower orders." The writings of Ignatius Donnelly, a bankrupt land speculator and greenbacker critic of railroads whose bid for a congressional seat narrowly failed in 1878, typify the fixation on catastrophe. Donnelly attributed his personal difficulties to a conspiracy of financiers and foresaw disaster for the United States. He wrote two books, *Atlantis* and *Ragonark: The Age of Fire and Gravel,* the former a treatise to prove the existence of the legendary island, the latter to demonstrate that cataclysms facilitated world development. In 1891

Donnelly wrote the apocalyptic *Caeser's Column,* a novel that spins conspiracy theory upon conspiracy theory in the story of a megalopolis run by plutocrats mad with power and profit. Eventually the proletariat at the bottom of the economic pyramid revolt, a quarter of a million dead are piled upon Caeser's column, and the anarchic mob kills its own leaders. Although Donnelly ends the carnage by conjuring up an agrarian utopia in Uganda, the book is notable for its pessimistic vision of unrelieved hatred between scheming financial parasites and brutalized, and therefore brutal, producers.

If Donnelly, Adams, and Lease could be dismissed as eccentric or dyspeptic, William Dean Howells could not. A product of rural Ohio, Howells' fear of urbanization and industrial capitalism issued in the depiction of a simple farmer (*The Rise of Silas Lapham,* 1885) corrupted by wealth and the lure of effete Boston society. But the turning point came with the Haymarket Riot of 1886. Appalled at the unjust conviction of the Haymarket anarchists, Howells conducted a lonely struggle to prevent their executions. Impressed (through his reading of Tolstoy) with the teachings of Christian socialism, Howells became convinced that only a reform of capitalism could prevent industrial warfare. *A Hazard of New Fortunes* (1890), his greatest novel, indicted the nation's economic institutions amid an examination of virtually every major social philosophy: laissez-faire capitalism, socialism, anarchism, feudalism. Significantly, Howells, the perennial optimist who had saved Silas Lapham by returning him to the farm and who was to beseech writers to stress "the smiling aspects" of American life, found no easy solutions in this novel. He certainly sympathized with the sentiments expressed by Conrad Dryfoos, the book's Christian socialist: "It's we—people like me, of my class—who make the poor betray one another (as scabs)." But Conrad is unable to ease class antagonisms and, mute in the face of police brutality ("he could not speak, he could not move his tongue"), he is killed in the midst of a strike. The author's fictional alter ego, Basil March, watches the unfolding events in powerless horror, increasingly aware of his own fatalistic views. Death chastens the living, but the Dickensian tidiness of the ending cannot hide Howells' uncertainty about the future.

A major proponent of literary "realism," Howells defended the presentation of an analysis without a solution. the novelist, he believed, must present "things as they are" without filtering them through screens of allegory or moralism. Howells hoped readers could then act with accurate knowledge: realism was a call to action that did not provide a blueprint for change. Howells, whose passion for justice had been aroused by strike-breaking and the miseries of urban poverty, believed that industrial conflict could be avoided only by appealing to the collective wisdom and compassion of Americans. But in the late nineteenth century Howells shivered with anxiety.

The historian Frederick Jackson Turner, like Howells, was not given to apocalyptic visions. Yet he too feared that America's unique immunity from class strife had ended. In "The Significance of the Frontier in American History" (1893) Turner argued that the extraordinary degree of economic and political egalitarianism in America depended upon the availability of free land. The West had served as a safety valve, draining off discontent by providing urban workers with a place to start anew—often as independent farmers. A permanent proletariat ripe for revolution had not developed in the United States, as it had in Europe, because young men, in Horace Greeley's immortal phrase, could "go West." On the frontier, Turner asserted, rough equality existed: the gap between the wealthy and the poor was relatively narrow and people were valued for their ability rather than for their name or past. Mobility, opportunity, and democracy reinforced one another and provided stability and prosperity.

The census of 1890, Turner pointed out, announced that the frontier was closed. The implications of the disappearance of America's landed heritage needed little adumbration to depression-conscious Americans in 1893. Early in the twentieth century, as Richard Hofstadter has noted (*The Progressive Historians Turner, Beard, Parrington,* 1968), Turner was more explicit: social conflict might well increase because the safety valve was closed, "classes are becoming alarmingly distinct," and prejudices of native-born employers and workers against immigrants were intensifying. Unless the nation found "frontiers of better social domains yet unexplored," Turner warned, cities might explode when workers realized that they and their children were factory slaves.

Although Turner's essays were not widely distributed at the turn of the century, more popular writers had anticipated his thesis. Josiah Strong's *Our Country* (1885) reflected the fears of Protestant clergymen who, as Henry May has demonstrated (*The Protestant Churches and Industrial America,* 1949), were shaken out of their complacency by the labor violence of the 1870s and 1880s. Strong's book, a powerful jeremiad addressed to Anglo-Saxon Protestants, linked the strength and stability of the nation's institutions to the availability of free land: "When the supply is exhausted, we shall enter upon a new era and shall more rapidly approximate European conditions of life." Race, ethnicity, and class fused in Strong's troubled mind; an ominous mass of nonwhite, non-Anglo-Saxon, non-Christian people mired in poverty loomed on the horizon, blocking the sun like a cloud of locusts. Unless drastic action was taken, plagues might continue to descend upon the United States.

Concern about impending social conflict sometimes resulted in reform prescriptions that sought to promote democracy and equity by preventing the "robber barons" from taking unfair advantage of the producing class. Antipathy to parasitic speculators and bankers who preyed on hard-working farmers—a classic American theme shared by Puritans, Jeffersonians, and Jacksonians—grew in the Gilded Age because industrialism had given finance capitalists more power. Reformers attributed the arrogance of bankers, businessmen, and landlords to a confidence that the working-class producers of wealth— divided by race, religion, and ethnicity, mesmerized by the ideology of equal opportunity, awed by the "genius" of the wealthy—could not identify their enemies, let alone unite against them. The first task of radicals and reformers, then, was mass education: the sources of oppression must be exposed and the people made aware of their political power and responsibilities. In a political culture where numbers counted, the government could become an instrument of social justice.

With these aims in mind, several critics sought to pinpoint the inequities in the American economy. Henry George's *Progress and Poverty* (1879), which sold more than two million copies, asserted that a "single tax" would permanently avert depression, restore equality of opportunity, and break the power of the speculators. Since landlords did not deserve the "unearned increment" they received from rent, such money should revert to the public through a tax on unproductive or underused land. The tax would generate sufficient revenue to enable the government to end all other forms of taxation. George believed that the "single tax," by ending the accumulation of unearned wealth, would stimulate growth and reward "productive" capital and labor. In the 1880s George spearheaded a single tax political campaign that culminated in a close but unsuccessful race for mayor of New York City.

The popularity of *Progress and Poverty* may be due to its ability to combine a specific reform program with a distrust of government authority. Although George opposed monopolies and advocated government ownership of "natural monopolies," e.g., public utilities, he hoped to preserve laissez-faire capitalism and nourish freedom of opportunity. The "single tax" was wonderfully simple, a patent medicine cure for all ailments. It abolished the rentier class in a single stroke, and promised to return the land to the producers. Paul Boller points out (*American Thought in Transition: The Impact of Evolutionary Naturalism, 1865–1900,* 1969) that George thought his approach was the capitalist's last ditch. The single tax would

raise wages, increase the earnings of capital, extirpate pauperism, abolish poverty, give remunerative employment to whoever wishes it, afford free scope to human powers, elevate morals, and taste, and intelligence, purify government and carry civilization to yet nobler heights. . . .

These noble aims, George believed, could be achieved without governmental regulations that would sap the initiative of a Ragged Dick or an Andrew Carnegie. Economic differences there would always be, but George was convinced that the "single tax," by equating success with ability and enterprise, provided the basis of social harmony.

Unlike George, Edward Bellamy, who identified competition and profit as the causes of human misery and social conflict, called for an end to capitalism in the United States. His utopian novel, *Looking Backward, 2000–1887* (1888), described the nation's classless society of the year 2000, in an effort to convince Americans that the elimination of institutions that rewarded greed would make poverty obsolete. In this utopian society every citizen was an employee of the government, which required men and women between the ages of twenty-one and forty-five to serve in the national "Industrial Army." The tentacles of government reached everywhere: health care, education, and welfare services were available to all and citizens received credit tickets ($4,000 a year in value) to purchase other goods and services. Depression and an economy of scarcity had given way to a harvest of abundance, because satisfied laborers, brimming with patriotic fervor, produced more although they worked fewer hours.

Although the new society abolished classes and sought to cultivate individualism, critics charged that Bellamy's utopia was hierarchical and authoritarian, a gigantic regiment of workers in service to the state. If classes based on wealth were gone, invidious distinctions based on rank in government service remained. Bellamy, in fact, had anticipated charges of excessive regimentation; the utopian state allowed all citizens to choose their occupations after a brief basic training. All had complete freedom to use credit tickets in any way at all. Perhaps most importantly, citizens could retire to a life of leisure at forty-five or, at reduced pay, at thirty-five. The system, explained Dr. Leete to Julian West, the novel's Rip Van Winkle, is "elastic enough to give free play to every instinct of human nature which does not aim at dominating others or living on the fruits of others' labor." Equal distribution of material resources encouraged rather than stifled human energy, initiative, and creativity.

The enormous popularity of *Looking Backward* launched Bellamy on a campaign to bring the cooperative commonwealth to the United States well before the year 2000. The conditions that prompted the "Great Bloodless Revolution" described in the novel seemed to exist in Bellamy's America: capitalism had spawned a greater and greater concentration of wealth and power in the hands of monopoly capitalists. All that remained was for the majority to demand socialism and compel the plutocrats, who would doubtless see the vast numbers arrayed against them, to capitulate. To this end Bellamy organized "Nationalist Clubs" and sought popular support for his plan to manage the United States as a giant cooperative trust. The clubs, however, were often polite discussion societies that had difficulty attracting the urban masses. Before the end of the century they disappeared and Bellamy shifted his support to the Populists, who seemed to be the last best hope of the cooperative commonwealth.

Unwilling to wait until 2000 for the withering away of monopolistic finance captalism, the Populists sought to use the ballot box to "give Americans prosperity, that the man who creates shall own what he creates; to take the robber class from the throat of industry; to take possession of the government of the United States...." The Populists sought a coalition of "the toiling masses," a union of farmers and urban workers that would overwhelm the plutocrats by dint of sheer numbers. In the famous Omaha Platform of 1892, the Populists proclaimed their political philosophy: "We believe that the powers of government—in other words, the people—should be expanded—to the end that oppression, injustice and poverty shall eventually cease in the land." Their advocacy of railroad regulation, an income tax, postal savings bank, a federal subtreasury plan, and direct election of senators was truly radical in late nineteenth-century America. The Populist attempt to forge an alliance of the producing classes failed for a number of reasons: racial and ethnic prejudice, as we have seen, divided the movement; differences between "independent" farmers and industrial "wage slaves" over issues like the tariff and inflation emerged; bankers and manufacturers stepped up their support of the Republican party; and fusion necessitated the subordination of Populist principles to the goal of "free silver." With the defeat of William Jennings Bryan in 1896 the Populist comet disappeared from view.

The defeat of the Populists, it should be added, did not eradicate the fear of social conflict in America, as an exchange between Andrew D. White and the famed sociologist Lester Frank Ward makes clear. Writing former president White of Cornell University, who thought the Populist party "socialistic," "anarchistic," and a product of the "hatred of classes," Ward branded populism the intellectual child of Henry George's "vaporizings" and Edward Bellamy's "sugar-coated bomb." "I see, like you, nothing but disaster and reaction as the result of the possible success of this blind mob." Yet Ward confessed that he could take little solace from the defeat of Bryan: "I shall still regard it as but the foam from a deep current that has not ceased to flow and will not cease until it is strong enough to carry the world with it...." Ward's evolutionary pessimism was shared by many of his contemporaries. Populism was gone but not forgotten—a portent, perhaps, of a time when wealth and property would be seized by the government in the name of the people.

Socialists were certain that the Single Taxers, Bellamyite Nationalists, and Populists had faltered because they refused to accept the realities of industrial capitalism. The logic of capitalism, Marx had shown, necessitated ever-greater concentrations of power in the hands of the few who controlled the means of production, and an ever-widening chasm between the rich and the poor. Class lines would harden and human misery would increase—until the workers seized the factories and farms and abolished institutions based on profit. The "ruling class," however, would never peacefully allow the democratic majority to make the government the servant of the people. The key error of well-intentioned reformers, socialists insisted, was the failure to recognize that the government was merely the political arm of the ruling class. Any fair examination of government policies provided incontrovertible proof: who initiated and benefited from tariffs, free gifts of land to railroads, and the use of federal troops to break up strikes? Daniel DeLeon, the leader of the Socialist Labor Party, summed up the socialist view of government: "Since the birth of the ruling class, government has been the special prop of that very class. . . . The main function of the government of the ruling class today, apart from the continuous and increasingly difficult function of keeping the ruled class under, is to act as a breakwater against legislation that threatens danger to capitalism, or is at all distastefull to it." Neither Populist electoral exertions nor bloodless revolutions would result in a transfer of power from the ruling class to the workers. Only a class-conscious mass movement, willing to meet violence with violence and prepared to destroy capitalism root and branch, could bring power to the people.

Despite brave assertions that an "American species of socialism is inevitable," the efforts of DeLeon, Eugene V. Debs, I.W.W. organizer William D. Haywood, and others to build a massive socialist coalition ended in failure. Accounting for this failure has become a popular pastime of historians. Certainly, as Daniel Bell has noted (*Marxian Socialism in the United States,* 1952), American ideals and opportunities weakened the appeal of socialism. The individualistic philosophy of Alger, open frontiers, a relatively high standard of living, and the absence of a fixed social hierarchy based on heredity convinced Americans that success was possible. "On the reefs of roast beef and apple pie," argued German Social Democrat Werner Sombart, "socialist utopias of every sort are sent to their doom." Although mobility was not nearly as widespread as historians once imagined, this edifice of American expectations, though a bit shaken, still stood at the end of the nineteenth century.

Bell's central thesis that American socialists misunderstood the essence of politics, that they shirked the problem of living in the world by refusing to make moral absolutes relevant to particular demands with the fewest necessary compromises, is not persuasive. More often than not, the dilemma for radicals was how, not whether, to support reforms that would benefit workers. Both labor leader Eugene V. Debs and Bill Haywood won support by focusing upon industrial conditions. DeLeon, who expelled his son Solon from the Socialist Labor party for heresies about the Marxian labor theory of value, also vigorously supported minimum wage and maximum hours legislation and woman suffrage, although he steadfastly claimed that the ruling class had barred "the government gate" against such reforms. Bell admits that the program of the Socialist Democratic party anticipated much New Deal legislation. Because they were radical outsiders with little power, socialists had to perform a precarious balancing act: they had to influence the political process without legitimizing it; they had to be effective and responsive enough to attract a mass constituency without sacrificing long-term goals to short-term interests. Fusing theory and practice was difficult, not because socialists avoided the political maelstrom, but because they descended into it.

The peculiar composition of the American labor force may help explain the failure of socialism. Massive immigration, as we have seen, contributed to a singularly heterogeneous and mobile work force. Many immigrants came to the United States with the hope that they could earn money and return home with sufficient capital to purchase land. Such people made poor recruits in the socialist army. A Slavic steelworker described his goals: "a good job, save money, work all time, go home, sleep, no spend." Frequently, immigrants did not bring their families to the New World (in 1870 only 4,574 of the 63,199 Chinese in America were women), nor were they necessarily in search of equality, democracy, and political freedom. Horatio Alger, in a sense, had relevance to them and, for those who did not "make it," a safety valve existed. The proportion of immigrants who returned home increased markedly at the turn of the century. We cannot accurately estimate how many left in despair but those who departed were not likely to have sustained efforts to alter American capitalism.

Those who stayed may also have weakened class solidarity. Perpetual wanderers, they often roamed, like Jurgis Rudkus of Upton Sinclair's *The Jungle* (1906), from city to town to countryside, accepting work wherever they could find it. Rootless immigrants and restless natives made for a society of astonishing transience. Stephan Thernstrom has estimated (*The Other*

Bostonians, 1973) that only half of the population living in a community at a given time could be found there ten years later. Perpetual motion made the construction of organizations based on trust and the articulation of common goals more difficult. Ghettoes, moreover, divided workers into enclaves of wary, even warring nationalities. If class consciousness grew not only from common experiences at work, but from interaction in the community, then ethnic segregation may have undermined unity based on class as it reinforced national identity.

Efforts to subordinate racial allegiances to class alliances limited the appeal of socialism to blacks. Because they denounced bigotry as a capitalist conspiracy to divide workers, socialists maintained that race prejudice would wither away once economic exploitation had been abolished. "There is nothing easier, nor yet more useless," DeLeon wrote, "than to discover the difference there is between a Negro and a white man." Negro laborers will never "successfully agitate for their separate emancipation" until and unless they unite with other workers. The color line, like sex or nationality lines, "disrupts; the class line solidifies the revolutionary forces of our generation." Because socialists insisted that the "Negro problem" was a problem of class, David Shannon points out (*The Socialist Party of America,* 1955), the Socialist party refused to propose any programs exclusively designed for blacks. Nor were socialists free of race prejudice. Although Victor Berger admitted that "the system" degraded Negroes, his public statements hardly encouraged biracial cooperation:

There can be no doubt that the negroes and mulattoes constitute a lower race—that the Caucasian and even the Mongolian have the start on them in civilization by many thousand years—so that negroes will find it difficult ever to overtake them. The many cases of rape which occur wherever negroes are settled in large numbers prove, moreover, that the free contact with the whites has led to the further degeneration of the negroes, as well as all other inferior races.

Although socialist William English Walling helped found the NAACP, the policy of the Socialist party remained that the end of wage slavery provided the only solution of the race question.

The attitude of the Socialist party toward ethnicity was more complex, but not much more satisfactory. The party bowed to the persistence of ethnic group loyalty by permitting foreign language socialist federations to affiliate with the Socialist party. The federations remained autonomous, with full power to set dues and policy, and to run meetings in their native tongues. Cracks in the socialist front appeared often, especially when members debated U.S. participation in World War I. More importantly, socialists could not agree on an immigration policy. On one hand some believed that class lines crossed national boundaries; unrestricted immigration therefore should be supported. Others stressed that immigrant greenhorns, who were often willing to work for low wages, strengthened capitalism. What should be done? Most socialists agreed that stopping "the yellow peril" was in the interest of American labor, but could not resolve their differences about European immigration. The 1910 Socialist party "platform" on immigration tried to be all things to all people but it probably did little to attract immigrants to the party:

The Socialist Party favors all legislative measures tending to prevent the immigration of strike-breakers and contract laborers, and the mass importation of workers from foreign countries, brought about by the employing classes for the purpose of weakening the organization of American labor, and of lowering the standard of life of American workers.

The party is opposed to the exclusion of any immigrants on account of their race or nationality, and demands that the United States be at all times maintained as a free asylum for all men and women persecuted by the governments of their countries on account of their politics, religion or race.

Responsive to its large immigrant constituency, this socialist position nevertheless did not solve the riddle of ethnic differences.

Racial and ethnic heterogeneity and the transience of laborers were not the only problems that bedeviled socialists. Immigrants may also have prevented working-class solidarity in an even more indirect way. In taking low-paying, low-status factory jobs, immigrants pushed native laborers up into the middle class. The success of the natives, who rarely expressed gratitude to their inadvertent benefactors, sustained their belief in industrial capitalism. The obstacles to socialism, then, were many and powerful, although radicals won a few adherents and, as we have seen, many observers remained haunted by the spectre of class conflict. With the future still in doubt, twentieth-century reformers searched for ideas and programs that recognized economic interest as a wellspring of human action, but promised progress through a gradual, orderly alteration of the relationship among workers, government, and corporations.

Unwilling to embrace revolutionary socialism but still wary of governnent, many workers turned to labor unions by the end of the nineteenth century. More and more the American labor movement accepted capitalism, and the permanent existence of a class of industrial workers; union leaders sought higher wages and better working conditions for their members, who could expect to live and die as members of the working class. Strong unions, that limited the power of corporations through healthy competition but recognized that labor and management must cooperate to insure continued prosperity for all, provided the best protection for workers. Industrial capitalism, union leaders asserted, fostered the interdependence of worker and manufacturer: each contributed to the prosperity of all; all should expect an increasing share of the growing abundance.

Samuel Gompers, a founder and for four decades the leader of the American Federation of Labor, became convinced that the interests of workers could best be served by nonrevolutionary trade unions that accepted industrial capitalism. The Knights of Labor, the national labor union in the 1870s and 1880s, had faltered, he believed, because of its utopian belief that members could become independent enterpreneurs (Gerald Grob, *Workers and Utopia,* 1961). Thus the Knights wasted precious resources in chimerical schemes to purchase factories and mines that the members themselves would operate. Terence Powderly, leader of the Knights of Labor, opposed strikes, which he thought ineffective and not useful to his ultimate goals, and often enraged workers faced with low wages when he advised them to quit in protest and/or move West. Gompers shed such utopian dreams (and the socialism of his youth) in favor of a trade unionist philosophy wrapped in a pay envelope. Indeed a labor movement concerned exclusively with wages and working conditions seemed well suited to the United States, for in a nation that achieved universal manhood suffrage without a struggle, workers were concerned far more with economic security than with political rights. The professedly apolitical unionism of Gompers, Selig Perlman asserted (*A Theory of the Labor Movement,* 1928), appealed to workers with "a long heritage of faith in the existing political system, if not the prevailing economic order."

Workers, said Gompers, "are a distinct and practically permanent class of modern society." Because industrial capitalism was also a permanent feature of American society, labor must press for immediate gains rather than revolutionary change: "more, more, here and now." Individualism must give way to collective bargaining, and if necessary, collective actions such as strikes and boycotts. The AFL, organized by craft and subdivided according to geography, provided the structure for effective bargaining. Unity in numbers, Gompers asserted, was the hallmark of a successful trade union: "Numbers give confidence not only to members but to outsiders." If the union did not provide an exit from the working class, it promised higher wages, improved safety conditions, and perhaps fewer hours on the job.

Such goals, however, necessitated an abandonment of radicalism, and Gompers spent much of his career combatting socialist infiltration into the AFL. The substantial socialist strength in the union surfaced in the adoption of a resolution, for the "consideration" of affiliated unions, calling for the collective ownership of the means of production. In 1893 the membership narrowly defeated a proposal to mandate "favorable consideration" of this statement. The following year Gompers engineered the repeal of this resolution, although it cost him the union presidency for one year. When he returned to power, he systematically ended socialist "boring from within," thereby consolidating his control of AFL organization and policy. By the early twentieth century Gompers was the undisputed prime spokesman for a small but growing trade union movement. He accepted bigness in economics as "natural" and asserted that only strong unions could check the trusts. Gompers also recognized the crucial role to be played by government in aiding workers. In 1906 the AFL Washington lobbyists presented "Labor's Bill of Grievances" to Congress and President Theodore Roosevelt. The union demanded a rigorously enforced, eight-hour law for government employees, prohibition of convict labor in private industry, exemption of unions from antitrust laws, and immigration restriction—and threatened to oppose politicians who voted against this program. Reform, of course, did not come easily or quickly, and the press denounced the AFL's demands for "a class Congress and a class judiciary," but the significance of the emergence of this new interest group was not lost on politicians (Harold Livesay, *Samuel Gompers and Organized Labor in America,* 1978). Despite his insistence that his purge of socialists and his forays into politics were based on "practical" rather than "theoretical" concerns, Gompers' program was grounded in theory. "Business unionism," which also attracted many progressives, accepted the durability of capitalism and the permanence of an industrial working class, and sought gains for labor within existing political and economic institutions.

This philosophy of unionism also had an academic champion, John R. Commons, the labor historian and progressive, who saw salvation for workers in the organization of a "bargaining class" to represent their interests. Commons, Alan Dawley has argued (*Class and Community: The Industrial Revolution in Lynn,* 1976), sought to transfer "class conflict out of the arena of irreconcilable struggle" and to the bargaining table, where both sides could win. "Recognition of social classes," he argued in a paper delivered at the 1899 session of the American Economic Association, "means self-government based on legalized justice between classes.'' Such recongition, moreover, should be accompanied by increased responsibilities for labor leaders in government: "What is needed is a representative assembly which will bring together these leaders with the leaders of all other classes, so that they can make similar (mutually beneficial) compromises in politics." Commons consequently proposed a national assembly where labor, business and farmers would choose their own representatives. Like Gompers, John R. Commons believed that the recognition of unions as a permanent and legitimate interest group would "protect business and the nation," promote social harmony, and provide workers with a fair share of American abundance.

As union leaders and rank and file gauged the benefits of collective action, progressive reformers drew together several strands of social thought to advocate interest group competition, supervised and regulated by a neutral government and mitigated by civic and national loyalty, as the best guarantee of prosperity and inter-class harmony. Historians have noted the anomaly of progressivism, a movement[1] for change amidst the good times of the early twentieth century. Progressives, however, had not forgotten the strife of the Gilded Age, nor could they—since muckraking journalists continually exposed corporate "excesses" and political corruption to public scrutiny. The progressives sensed that theirs was the ideal time to promote "industrial democracy," a system based on the sharing of power and profit by workers and capitalists. They accepted as dicta the assertions by newly professionalized social scientists that Spencerian individualism was a fossil of the Darwinist jungle, that the group was the fundamental unit of society and that government could effectively mediate disputes between groups. None expressed these views more clearly than Theodore Roosevelt:

A simple and poor society can exist as a democracy on a basis of sheer individualism. But a rich and complex industrial society cannot so exist; for some individuals, and especially those artificial individuals

[1]Peter Filene, as noted, doubts that a "movement" existed.

called corporations, become so very big that the ordinary in-dividual...cannot deal with them on terms of equality. It therefore becomes necessary for these ordinary individuals to combine in their turn, first in order to act in their collective capacity through that biggest of all combinations called the government, and second, to act, also in their own self-defense, through private combinations, such as farmers' associations and trade unions.

Although Roosevelt recognized that "aside from their general interest as citizens, special groups of citizens have special inter-ests," he sought unity among contending economic and social groups. While it is sometimes necessary, "from both a legislative and social standpoint," he said, "to consider men as a class," in the long run "it is impossible for a democracy to endure if the political lines are drawn to coincide with class lines." Although few were as explicit as he, many progressives shared both Roosevelt's fear of class politics and his appreciation of interest-group politics.

Most of the time, progressives assured themselves, the pro-ductive friction generated by the bargaining process would yield an agreement. If, however, negotiations stalled, government would step in, secure in the belief that because it was truly rep-resentative and therefore neutral, it commanded the loyalty of all the "bargaining classes."

Social scientists agreed that the self-reliant individual living in isolated majesty was extinct—if, indeed, such a person ever lived. Because human beings were social by instinct and inclina-tion, they insisted, groups based on intimate association or mu-tual self-interest would always form. The true test of a society was its ability to promote intergroup cooperation. The alterna-tive was "a mosaic of little worlds which touch but do not inter-penetrate," wary, suspicious worlds forever at war.

A preoccupation of American intellectuals at the end of the nineteenth century, Jean Quandt (*From the Small Town to the Great Community,* 1970), R. Jackson Wilson (*In Quest of Com-munity: Social Philosophy in the United States, 1860-1920,* 1968), and Paul Boyer (*Urban Masses and Public Order in America,* 1978) have argued, was the search for loyalty and for social harmony amidst heterogeneity. Recognizing that the old ties of community that characterized small town America had been dissolved by the acid of industrialism, they sought to fashion a science of environmental change that molded individuals by recognizing the strength and validity of group consciousness and organization.

Charles Horton Cooley, sociologist at the University of Michigan, was certain that human experience could be understood only as social experience. The "self" was a product of the social environment; "individuals" and "society" were simply aspects of the same thing. In *Human Nature and the Social Order* (1902) Cooley focused on the "primary group" as the key factor in value formation:

By primary group I mean those characterized by intimate face-to-face association and cooperation. They are primary in several senses, but chiefly in that they are fundamental in forming the social nature and ideals of the individual. The result of intimacy, psychologically, is a certain fusion of individualities in a common whole, so that one's very self . . . is the common life and purpose of the group.

Morality, then, was the standard regarded as normal by the "primary group." Cooley was concerned, however, that the circle of persons who constituted the primary group for a ghetto dweller or a factory worker might not be morally wholesome. To redirect and reverse "degenerative tendencies," Cooley sought to enlist the very technology that had produced alienation and anomie. By using mass communication, for example, social planners could reinforce the "warm and fresh" aspects of "group consciousness," for if allowed full expression, human nature would bring individuals into harmony with healthy group norms. By contrast, if the debilitating environment of poverty and prejudice continued to check the "natural" tendencies of individuals, rigid, self-interested economic classes characterized by "a complacent ignorance" would certainly result. The organization of groups, then, was inevitable, but only a conscious program of positive environmentalism could insure a harmonious society of mutual respect.

University of Wisconsin sociologist E. A. Ross, in contrast to Cooley, urged "social control" of the masses. Like so many of his contemporaries, Ross blamed industrialism for "drawing apart into opposing camps...rich and poor, capitalist and worker. . . ." An invincible opponent of laissez-faire, Ross believed that society must act—or drift into class conflict. In *Social Control* (1901) Ross showed that the evolution of Western society from a relatively static, homogeneous order to a stratified, culturally fragmented urban industrial civilization had removed many of the bulwarks against social conflict. To replace them, Ross called for a "Social Religion" that would convince the masses that "a bond of ideal relationship between the members of. . .society" existed. Ross, who made no effort to hide his contempt for non-Aryans, believed that churches and schools could mold immigrants and other members of the "lower orders": "The passiveness of the average mind will make it safe to weave into. . .moral instruction certain convenient illusions and fallacies which it is nobody's interest to denounce." In his less Machiavellian moments, however, Ross hoped for a world where the loyalty, affection, and responsibility of the primary group would be writ large, not by coercion, but through the efforts of an "ethical elite," "unspoiled by class spirit," to construct a moral consensus that transcended the selfish, ignorant parochialism of race, class, and ethnicity.

While Cooley and Ross (albeit in very different ways) sought a spirit of loyalty to transform individuals and interest groups into smoothly functional social components, Lester Frank Ward, "the father of American sociology," discredited laissez faire by challenging the assuption that unregulated competition insured the "survival of the fittest." Since Social Darwinists used the term "natural" to describe phenomena they approved, he charged, "survival of the fittest" was little more than a tautology: the "fittest" was defined by examining those who survived. Superior strains of fruit trees, cereals, and domestic cattle came from carefully controlled growth and breeding, proof that regulation, not competition, provided the best results. Ward agreed, argues Richard Hofstadter (*Social Darwinism in American Thought,* 1944), that corporate organizations were "natural," that to break them up would destroy "the integrated organisms of social evolution"; but he went on to say that "positive legislation" to insure fair competition was therefore all the more necessary. Perhaps natural selection had once helped the human race, but now human advancement dictated that "natural" law give way to "the improvement of society by cold calculation." Rational planning, if supplemented by education to bring "the promise and potency of a higher life" [to] those "swarming, spawning millions, the bottom layer of society, the proletariat, the working class...nay, even the denizens of the slums. . ." would equalize opportunity by removing unfair advantage and release human action for socially beneficial deeds.

While Ward championed positive legislation, the brilliant and eccentric anthropologist-economist Thorstein Veblen demolished the doctrine of the survival of the fittest. In *The Theory of the Leisure Class* (1899), Veblen launched a sustained and sarcastic attack on "the captains of industry." The successful man, he claimed, usually possessed "cupidity, prudence, and chicane" in abundant doses and a temperament compatible to "petty intrigue and nugatory subtleties." The leisure class exalted laziness as a virtue (canes and white gloves were badges of conscious indolence), spent money to show that they had money to spend (Veblen coined the term "conspicuous consumption"), and instigated wars to amuse themselves. Veblen's message was clear: if "natural selection" produced this odious group of parasites, then society must seize control of evolution, and direct it to more equitable and productive purposes.

If Veblen could be dismissed as an eccentric malcontent (he had been dismissed from several universities for sexual "indiscretions"), the "New Economists" led by Richard T. Ely could not. Ely was one of scores of bright young Americans who had returned from German universities in the late nineteenth century prepared to dethrone the regnant dogma of unregulated competition. "The final victory of man's machinery over nature's control of human society," Simon Patten asserted, "was the transition from anarchic and puny individualism to the group acting as a powerful, intelligent organism." In 1884 the new economists organized the American Economic Association (AEA), which they hoped to use as a platform to denounce laissez-faire.

Ely, the first secretary of the AEA, became the most prominent spokesman for the "new economics." Orthodox economists, he charged, began and ended with a single refrain: "hands off." By contrast, the new economics accounted for ever-changing social circumstances; economic policy must change as society changed. Ely preferred a mixed economy that combined the best features of capitalism and socialism, but was premeated with the ideal of Christian brotherhood. Like Cooley, he applauded the interdependence of industrial America because it promoted fraternity. Even more than Ward, Ely insisted that government become an active watchdog over the economy. State income and real estate taxes, and government ownership of "natural" monopolies, would prevent individual and corporate excesses and protect consumers. Economists, in short, must be flexible social scientists prepared to limit competition and increase government activity.

Although Ely feared class conflict, he expressed sympathy for labor unions. They were the workers' only protection against the corporate octopus, whose tentacles—yellow-dog contracts, blacklists, Pinkertons—were long and powerful. Ely's ultimate vision of Christian brotherhood was designed to prevent labor organizations from becoming fertile ground for class hatred. Indeed, as Benjamin Rader has noted (*The Academic Mind: The Influence of Richard T. Ely in American Life,* 1967), Ely believed that the best unions elevated the working class mentally, morally, and monetarily by providing libraries, advocating temperance, and assessing fines for profanity. Class differences were best dealt with by supporting responsible institutions to mediate disputes. And on those rare occasions that management and labor remained at odds, Ely expected government to be ready with the machinery of arbitration. Although Ely's reform spirit flagged at times during his long life, he continued to hope that self-interest and the Christian gospel of fraternity would make workers and capitalists responsible, if not friendly, antagonists.

Many progressives sought to translate the findings of social science into public policy. Out of genuine concern over corporate gluttony and working-class deprivation, they sought to democratize the economy by regulating trusts, improving working conditions, widening educational opportunities and giving laborers "an active concern in the ends that control their activity." Workers, a progressive "vanguard" asserted, had the same right as capitalists to organize responsible groups to represent their interests. Yet even these reformers hastened to add that every American recognizes higher moral responsibilities than simple, selfish allegiance to economic class. A neutral, truly representative state, an industrial democracy willing to break down barriers to equal opportunity, would command the loyalty of all by providing stability through prosperity. Economic stratification might indeed be inevitable, but the abundance generated by industrial capitalism could lift the bottom of society, while building a bridge to the middle class for anyone with the will and ability to cross it. The progressives sought a harmonious community, where individuals were interchangeable parts, able to move from class to class, while classes were permanent but indispensable to the good of the whole.

Most progressives, contends George Mowry (*The Era of Theodore Roosevelt and the Birth of Modern America, 1900–1912,* 1958), condemned economic classes as "greedy," "arrogant," "insolent," "ruthless," "unsocial," and "tyrannical." Chester Roswell, a leading California progressive, spoke for his fellow reformers when he predicted that if class prejudice and class pride became predominant American liberty would be destroyed, peaceful reform impossible, and "nothing but revolution" would remain. Theodore Roosevelt agreed:

'I am for labor,' or 'I am for capital,' substitutes something else for the immutable laws of righteousness. The one and the other would let the class man in, and letting him in is the one thing that will most quickly eat out the heart of the Republic.

The wish, as expressed by a hero in a Harold Frederick novel, that "the abominable word 'class' could be wiped out of the English language as it is spoken in America," did not of course give birth to the fact, and the progressives sought programs to weaken class prejudice without forfeiting the wealth, efficiency, and power that flowed from corporate consolidation and labor organization.

The ghetto, in James Weinstein's apt metaphor, was the settlement workers' Galapagos, where they immersed themselves in problems of poverty. The philosophy of the settlement, wrote Jane Addams (*Twenty Years at Hull House,* 1910), rested "on the solidarity of the human race." But to ignore the differences between classes and the legitimate needs of the working poor was to court disaster: "the good we secure for ourselves is precarious and uncertain, is floating in mid-air, until it is secured for all of us." Because the classes lived side by side, "without knowledge of each other, without fellowship," because the poor had no share "in the traditions and social energy which make for progress," they might well see anarchy and violence as the only form of relief. The very decision of settlement workers to live in the ghetto, Addams believed, demonstrated that sympathy cut across class lines and that social relations could be transformed by conscious and deliberate effort.

The voluntary efforts of self-directed individuals, however, had to be accompanied by government policies designed to remove handicaps caused by the accident of birth. Consequently the settlement workers agitated for tenement house laws, neighborhood parks, maximum hours, and factory safety regulations. By converting schools into community centers, they hoped to provide an alternative to the saloonkeeper, the prostitute, the urban boss, and the radical demagogue, who fed on the despair of the powerless. Most importantly the settlement workers sought to open public education to poor children by demanding child labor legislation, school lunch programs, school nurses, and by cajoling wary parents into sending their children to kindergarten. Sinclair Lewis chided the reformers for trying to interest the poor in irrelevant subjects: trout fishing, the eating of bran, the geography of Charlemagne's empire. Yet Lewis missed the point: aware that poverty trapped people in stultifying materialism, the settlement workers sought to awaken aesthetic and spiritual sensibilities to facilitate the transition to the middle class. In a sense the reformers tried to give substance to the Horatio Alger myth. If success *really* depended upon merit, and if all had a chance to reach their potential, then the promise of America would be fulfilled.

Many settlement workers nonetheless remained convinced that class divisions were permanent. While Addams prized "the exceptional young man or woman who reaches the college and university and leaves the neighborhood of his childhood behind him," she recognized that reformers must "work out a method and an ideal adapted to the immediate surrounding." If everyone could not escape the "lower class," the poor could best protect themselves by organizing into a "consciously effective group." While few followed Florence Kelley and Ellen Starr to the picket lines, many joined Jane Addams' defense of labor's right to organize. Although she deplored strikes and violence, Addams tried to put herself in the place of strikers "who have for years belonged to an organization devoted to securing better wages and a higher standard of living, not only for themselves, but for all men in their trade," and who see their efforts destroyed by scabs. Even though labor seemed "so sordid" much of the time, Addams nonetheless allowed unions to meet at Hull House and in 1910 organized relief efforts to aid the 40,000 workers on strike against Hart, Schaffner and Marx. The answer to industrial conflict lay not in the extermination of unions, but in the acceptance of arbitration by disinterested third parties or neutral government officials.

To promote fraternity, and to help insure that workers did not become "more unionists than Americans," settlement workers joined a progressive campaign to promote "civic loyalty." The reformers' use of this concept has been brilliantly described by Paul Boyer as the insistence "that the city was no mere chance accumulation of free-floating human atoms, but a cohesive, interconnected social organism that deserved, indeed demanded, the dedicated loyalty of all its constituent parts." Civic loyalty, they implied when they did not simply assert, transcended class, race, and ethnic loyalties. The city was now viewed less as a den of iniquity and more as a "well-ordered household" that watched over its citizens and asked all to contribute to collective betterment.

Civic pride could best be inculcated if a beautiful city was made the property of all. The progressives therefore sprinkled parks and playgrounds throughout the city and founded municipal improvement societies, whose members cleaned boulevards, planted shrubs on busy streets, and removed ugly billboards. George Burnap, landscape architect in Washington, D.C., designed parks to reflect class realities and prompt civic pride: in slums parks consisted mainly of open spaces so that workers fleeing the tenements "would feel that the city is bestowing upon them a bountiful gift." Landscaping and facilities should be better than that to which they are accustomed, yet not form "sufficient contrast to cause resentment." Middle-class parks must express "restraint" and "order" to counteract the tendency to ape the extravagances of the wealthy, while in upper-class parks liberty of design might be indulged. Others in the "City Beautiful Movement," less preoccupied than Burnap with social control, believed that physical beauty and order prompted a moral reformation in the citizenry: "to make us love our city we must make our city lovely." Progressives entered classrooms as well as parks in their call to "civic duty." Civics classes became an integral part of the curriculum for native-born Americans as well as immigrants. Civic loyalty was often set against the provincial selfishness of class interest: could anyone honestly choose materialism and strife over spirituality and harmony?

Nationalism, in essence, was civic loyalty on a larger scale. The "New Nationalism," Charles Forcey has noted (*The Crossroads of Liberalism,* 1961), became the creed of progressives located mainly on the eastern seaboard. Theodore Roosevelt was their leader, Herbert Croly their philosopher. In *The Promise of American Life* (1909) Croly argued that nationalism implied a social contract in which the people pledged fealty and service to the federal government in return for protection and the promotion of the general welfare. An efficient government must use "constructive discrimination" (e.g., corporate and inheritance taxes, expropriation of "natural" monopolies) to regulate the economy in behalf of the national interest. Excessive liberty and the laissez-faire doctines of Jeffersonian individualism, Croly insisted, had resulted in inequality and a morally and socially undesirable distribution of wealth and power. To restore equality and democracy while extending prosperity, government must act, not as a neutral umpire, but as the representative of the interests of the whole society; the national interest must transcend all other interests.

Croly expressed deep concern about the growth of organizations dedicated to "associated action for themselves and competition for their adversaries." Permanent—indeed, indispensable—features of industrial America, "powerful and unscrupulous and well-organized special interests" such as corporations and unions had to be checked by the superior power and "organization of the national interest." If not, these organizations of class selfishness might lock in mortal combat: "the vast incoherent mass of the American people is falling into social groups, which restrict and define the mental outlook and social experience of their members." Croly admitted that the corporations had had "the best of the situation" but noted with alarm that unions, increasing in numerical strength, were beginning "to use the suffrage to promote a class interest." Both organizations must be controlled and directed to serve national goals (in extreme instances Croly advocated replacing pernicious unions with government unions) because only loyalty to the State, based on a feeling of human brotherhood and grounded in increasing democracy and prosperity, could temper class selfishness.

For many progressives, World War I provided a golden opportunity to extend federal activism while deepening national loyalty. Compulsory military service, proclaimed one enthusiast, "is a melting pot which will . . . break down distinctions of race and class and mold us into a new nation and bring forth the new Americans." Few expected that interest group politics would disappear (in fact, administration spokesman George

Creel repeatedly denounced efforts to confuse issues of labor welfare and labor loyalty by calling into question the "patriotism" of workers), but most progressives hoped that war would demonstrate the primacy of the national interest.

In domestic affairs, progressive politicians, though they fell short of Croly's ideal, accepted an enlarged role for the federal government and the continued domination of economic life by modern social organizations. Theodore Roosevelt's handling of the Anthracite Coal Strike of 1902 provided a model case of this progressive method. When the owners adamantly refused to meet with representatives of the United Mine Workers, Roosevelt called the parties to the White House and with the aid of J. P. Morgan, the "great Mongul of Wall Street," convinced them to accept arbitration. The settlement gave the miners a 10 percent raise, reduced working hours to nine, permitted the owners to raise the price of coal 10 percent, and did not force recognition of the union. The President claimed that he had given capital and labor "a square deal"; he had certainly set the precedent that made the government a third partner in labor disputes. Most of Roosevelt's actions, despite his "trustbuster" nickname, committed the government to regulation and supervision over combinations in interstate commerce, "instead of relying on the foolish antitrust law." Roosevelt's celebrated prosecution of the Northern Securities Company was designed as a signal to corporations to cease immoral practices rather than as an effort to "prohibit all combinations." Despite the much-heralded differences between the "New Nationalism" and the "New Freedom," the policies of Woodrow Wilson did not differ markedly from those of Roosevelt (James Weinstein, *The Corporate Ideal in the Liberal State 1900–1918,* 1968). Perhaps more reluctantly than Roosevelt, Wilson admitted: "I dare say we will never return to the older order of individual competition." He was pleased when the Federal Trade Commission encouraged the establishment of trade and manufacturing associations and permitted the cooperation of firms engaged in the export trade. Wilson's support of the Clayton Antitrust Act (1914), which exempted unions from prosecution as "conspiracies in restraint of trade," moreover, won the accolades of Samuel Gompers, who dubbed the legislation "labor's Magna Carta." When in the same year the President appointed William Wilson of the United Mine Workers to the newly created post of Secretary of Labor, Gompers asserted that unions had won a "paramount voice" in government. Both Presidents Roosevelt and Wilson, then, committed the federal government to the protective, and at times disciplinary scrutiny of "the bargaining classes."

Most progressives, to be sure, were reluctant designers of the Industrial State, often with an antipathy to unions and the closed shop as "coercion from start to finish." They hoped, moreover, that workers and capitalists would cooperate voluntarily—through organizations like the aptly named National Civic Federation. The NCF, which boasted corporate giants and labor leaders like Gompers among its membership, offered to mediate labor disputes. The spirit of voluntarism, they believed, was much preferable to government coercion. The interests of capital and labor, insisted Seth Low, President of the NCF in 1907, were certainly not identical, but were reconcilable. James Gilbert has observed (*Designing the Industrial State,* 1972) that the progressives believed industrialism created new kinds of social classes: capital, management, labor, consumer. Yet they were also convinced that a community of interests existed and that a neutral government had a duty to prevent exploitation of the public by facilitating cooperation.

Progressive social thinkers had wrought subtle but significant changes in perceptions of class interest. The recognition that economic interest group organization was permanent and even legitimate, these social thinkers contended, did not lead to the conclusion that class conflict was justified or inevitable. Workers and the progressive vanguard had learned a lesson from the capitalists: in a collectivist age power grew out of organization. As labor and capital vied for a larger share of the profits, however, progressives insisted that they observe the rules of the game laid down by the government. Progressivism contained in embryo the New Deal "broker state" which accepted, even praised, "conflict" if contained within acceptable boundaries. Workers could make substantial gains, with the help of a sympathetic government, without resorting to violence. The foundation of the progressive edifice, however, was civic and national loyalty; class interest, at best mere materialism, at worst vile and violent rapaciousness, must be subordinated to the general welfare and the ideal of Christian fraternity. Nationalism and civic pride in a sense were secular versions of the Social Gospel; men and women must strive to transcend class interests. For the progressives, who had begun to believe that pluralistic friction might increase stability but who feared that excessive friction ignited the fires of class conflict, loyalty was the ultimate safety valve. Therefore they accepted organizations of racial, ethnic, and economic interest—but only if all recognized the greater "call" of civic and national duty. Not surprisingly, the *New Republic* reiterated this theme as World War I ended. In the decades to come, the editors wrote, "we shall require a subordination of class and sectional interests to the interests of the nation. . . . For what we are deciding is whether we are to have cooperation in this country or a future civil war, whether we are to erect our building on solid ground or to build it over a volcano."

While examining the regulatory legislation of the early twentieth century, Gabriel Kolko (*The Triumph of Conservatism,* 1963) has labelled progressivism "an effort to preserve the basic social and economic relations essential to a capitalist society," a triumph for the status quo. Regulation, he argues, was initiated by sophisticated businessmen and their political henchmen who sought federal intervention as a means to make the economy more stable, predictable, secure, and less vulnerable to anarchic competition. Regulatory agencies, moreover, were dominated by businessmen themselves. Kolko is persuasive in documenting the extensive participation of businessmen in Square Deal and New Freedom legislation and in contending that most progressives assumed that the general welfare could often best be served by aiding responsible corporations. Yet progressivism, as we have seen, was not merely a response to corporate calls for stability in marketing and financial affairs. The progressive movement, if an organized, coherent "movement" existed at all, had many foci. Settlement workers and social science theories are on the periphery of Kolko's analysis, yet the impetus for reform stemmed from them as well as from sophisticated businessmen. Although progressive social thinkers, like Kolko's businessmen, sought stability through reformed industrial capitalism, they sincerely believed that all classes would benefit from the changes they proposed. Walter Weyl, to cite a prominent example, wrote *The New Democracy* (1912) to counter the Marxian prediction of increasing misery for workers. The book's thesis was "progress through prosperity," an insistence that the United States had the capacity to use its surplus to create a true democracy and a higher culture available to all. Weyl advocated the gradual socialization of industry but, significantly, he believed progressivism had taken the first step in that direction. In their optimism progressives certainly overestimated their capacity to achieve "industrial democracy" without fundamentally altering political and economic institutions. Yet their achievements should not be minimized. In advocating government regulation of the economy, in accepting corporations and unions as legitimate institutions of industrial society, the progressives were the first modern liberals in America. Confident that a responsible industrial capitalism could generate more prosperity than any other economic system, they hoped to share its largesse with all classes.

Bibliographical Essay

RACE

The best general introduction to its subject is Thomas Gossett's *Race: The History of an Idea in America* (Dallas, 1963). Two fine studies of racial thought in the nineteenth century are John Haller's *Outcasts From Evolution* (Urbana, IL, 1971) and George Fredrickson's *The Black Image in the White Mind* (New York, 1971). Haller examines the effect of Darwinism on racial thought. Frederickson's brilliant book subtly traces changing attitudes toward blacks. the author examines racism and "romantic racialism" with unerring discernment. More recently Ronald

Takakis' *Iron Cages: Race and Culture in Nineteenth Century America* (New York, 1979) has provocatively argued that anxious whites, who feared the "dark" qualities within themselves, assigned them to other races. Counterparts to the white self-image, blacks lacked industry and moral restraint, Indians the principle of accumulation. Two monographs focus relentlessly on the more virulent racism of the late nineteenth century: Idus Newbys' *Jim Crow's Defense: Anti-Negro Thought in America* (Baton Rouge, 1965) and Claude Nolen's *The Negro's Image in the South: The Anatomy of White Supremacy* (Lexington, KY, 1967).

Among the many general surveys of the black experience in America, I have found two especially useful. John Hope Franklin's *From Slavery to Freedom: A History of American Negroes* (5th ed., New York, 1978) has justifiably become a classic. More recently Dwight Hoover's *The Red and the Black* (Chicago, 1976) has traced attitudes toward blacks and native Americans throughout U.S. history. Hoover's treatment of the findings of social scientists studying race is particularly illuminating.

For almost two decades historians have examined the racial politics of Reconstruction. The long-ignored work of W. E. B. Du Bois was rediscovered during the 1960s. Du Bois' *Black Reconstruction in America* (New York, 1935) refuted the "Dunning School" interpretation and offered a Marxist analysis of the period. During the 1960s most scholars emphasized the rampant racism of the period. Forrest G. Wood's often strident *Black Scare: The Racist Response to Emancipation and Reconstruction* documents the thesis presented in its title. In *The Right to Vote: Politics and the Passage of the Fifteenth Amendment* (Baltimore, 1965), William Gillette indicts the Radical Republicans for dumping black rights when the issue became a political liability. By contrast LaWanda Cox and John H. Cox, in *Politics, Principle and Prejudice: Dilemma of Reconstruction America* (Glencoe, IL, 1963), argue that the Republicans were not motivated primarily by idealism. The most balanced and the most persuasive treatment of late nineteenth century attitudes toward blacks is James McPherson's *The Abolitionist Legacy*

(Princeton, 1975). McPherson documents the continuing concern of abolitionists for the freedmen. This book should be read in conjunction with William S. McFeely's *Yankee Stepfather General O. O. Howard and the Freedmen* (New Haven, 1968), a sympathetic account of sincerity, naiveté, and blundering that is a virtual biography of the Freedmen's Bureau. Also useful in assessing the abolitionists is Henry Bullock's richly documented *A History of Negro Education in the South* (Cambridge, MA, 1967). Students who seek a more thorough acquaintance with George W. Cable should consult Arlin Turner's *George W. Cable: A Biography* (Durham, NC, 1956). Turner has also edited a book of Cable's essays, *The Negro Question.*

Whites, whether sympathetic or antagonistic to blacks, seldom fully understood the limited options of blacks in both the North and the South. Roger Ransom and Richard Sutch, in *One Kind of Freedom: The Economic Consequence of Emancipation* (Cambridge, England, 1977), label the consequence dire. Vernon Wharton's *The Negro in Mississippi 1865–1890* (Chapel Hill, NC, 1947) is a thorough examination of Reconstruction. C. Vann Woodward's *Strange Career of Jim Crow* (New York, 1955) unleashed a torrent of controversy with the assertion that some flexibility characterized race relations in the South before the 1890s. The argument rests heavily on the absence of Jim Crow legal statutes in the preceding decades. Woodward examines the responses to his thesis in "The Strange Career of a Historical Controversy," in *American Counterpoint* (Boston, 1971). Leon Litwack's elegantly written *Been in the Storm So Long* (New York, 1979) is a poignant, stirring account of the attempt of blacks to "overcome" during Reconstruction. Two studies focus on northern ghettoes. Seth M. Scheiner in *Negro Mecca: A History of the Negro in New York City 1865–1920* and Allan Spear in *Black Chicago: The Making of a Negro Ghetto 1890–1920* (Chicago, 1967) document the handicaps placed upon blacks but also chronicle attempts to break through economic, occupational, and cultural constraints.

Black nationalism and separatism attracted thousands of blacks in the late nineteenth century. The movements can often be correlated with the political or economic "bulldozing" of the period. Nell Painter's *The Exodusters* (New York, 1977) and Edwin Redkey's *Black Exodus: Black Nationalist and Back-to-Africa Movements, 1890–1910* (New Haven, 1969) sympathetically examine the enormous obstacles faced by migrating blacks. The student may wish to compare these early migrations to the massive effort headed by Marcus Garvey in the 1920s and should consult Edmund David Cronon's *Black Moses: The Story of Marcus Garvey and the Universal Negro Improvement Association* (Madison, 1955).

Biographies of black leaders provide an excellent source for historians of social thought. These leaders often both reflected and shaped the ideas of their constituents. August Meier's *Negro Thought in America, 1880–1915* (Ann Arbor, 1963) is a splendid analysis of tensions between accommodationism and self-help that gripped Frederick Douglass, Booker T. Washington, and others. A recent examination of the attitudes of black leaders toward race in an industrializing society is William Toll *The Resurgence of Race: Black Social Theory from Reconstruction to the Pan-African Conferences* (Philadelphia, 1979). Benjamin Quarles' *Frederick Douglass* (Washington, 1948) remains the standard work on the great abolitionist. Louis Harlan's *Booker T. Washington, The Making of a Black Leader 1856–1901* (New York, 1972) is a beautifully proportioned biography that illuminates the relationship between Washington and his white patrons. Harlan's "The Secret Life of Booker T. Washington," *Journal of Southern History* (1971), and "Booker T. Washington in Historical Perspective," *American Historical Review* (1970), supplement the biography. Washington's *Up From Slavery* (New York, 1901) is the best guide to the Tuskegee Wizard, but readers must bear in mind that it was aimed at a white audience. The two biographies of W. E. B. Du Bois, Francis L. Broderick's *W. E. B. Du Bois: Negro Leader in Time of Crisis* (Stanford, 1959) and Elliott Rudwick *W. E. B. Du Bois: A Study in Minority Group Leadership* (Philadelphia, 1960) are adequate, but a careful analysis of this great thinker's intellectual odyssey is still needed. Students should consult Du Bois' two autobiographies *Dusk of Dawn* (New York, 1940) and *Autobiography of W. E. B. Du Bois* (New York, 1968). Stephen Fox examines Du Bois' colleague in the Niagara Movement in *A Guardian of Boston, William Monroe Trotter* (New York, 1970). Rudwick's "The Niagara Movement," *Journal of Negro History* (1957), assesses the significance of the movement. Jervis Anderson's *A. Philip Randolph, A Biographical Portrait* (New York, 1972) breezes through the life but does not firmly set the labor leader in historical context.

Populist attitudes toward race must begin with C. Vann Woodward's masterpiece, *Thomas Watson: Agrarian Rebel* (New York, 1938). Woodward's magnum opus, *The Origins of the New South* (Baton Rouge, 1951), examines the influence of the ideology of race upon industrialization, southern politics, and agrarian reform in the years between Reconstruction and World War I. More recently Lawrence Goodwyn, in *Democratic Promise: The Populist Movement in America* (New York, 1976), has painstakingly reconstructed the social history of populism and has eloquently argued that the reformers often strove for interracial harmony. Readers should also consult J. Morgan Kousser's *The Shaping of Southern Politics* (New Haven, 1974) for a very careful analysis of the effects of disfranchisement on blacks and whites.

Most historians of political progressivism have detected little sympathy for blacks in the movement. This is especially true of progressive politicians. Rayford Logan's *The Betrayal of the Negro* (New York, 1965) chronicles the dismal story. George Sinkler's *The Racial Attitudes of American Presidents from Abraham Lincoln to Theodore Roosevelt* (New York, 1971) presents a similar thesis. Other useful sources include Dewey Grantham's "The Progressive Movement and the Negro" *South Atlantic Quarterly* (1955), Seth M. Scheiner's "Theodore Roosevelt and the Negro, 1901-1908," *Journal of Negro History* (1962) and Henry Blumenthal's "Woodrow Wilson and the Race Question," *Journal of Negro History* (1963).

Among the progressives, the settlement workers clearly evinced the greatest sympathy for black rights. The efforts are chronicled in Allen F. Davis' *Spearheads for Reform* (New York, 1967). Charles Flint Kellogg's *NAACP, Vol. 1, 1909–1920* also deals with the contribution of White reformers in the founding of the NAACP.

In addition to Hoover's *The Red and the Black* (Chicago, 1976), Wilcomb Washburn's *The Indian in America* (New York, 1975) and William Hagan's *American Indians* (Chicago, 1961) will introduce the reader to the tragic history of red-white relations. Inevitably these historians must rely primarily on white sources, and therefore our knowledge of native American perceptions of race is regrettably limited and conjectural.

The best book on white views of Indians is Robert Berkhofer's *The White Man's Indian* (New York, 1978). Berkhofer ambitiously covers the entire span of American history, but he manages also to set before the reader the spectrum of intellectual alternatives available to whites at a given historical moment.

Most historians have condemned white reformers for trying to destroy native American culture. Loring Priest's *Uncle Sam's Stepchildren: The Reformation of United States Indian Policy* (New Brunswick, NJ, 1942) is one such effort written in the wake of the Collier era in Indian affairs. Three more recent works treat the same era with varying degrees of sympathy for the reformers: Henry Fritz' *The Movement for Indian Assimilation 1860–1890* (Philadelphia, 1963), Robert Mardock's *The Reformers and the American Indian* (Columbia, MO, 1971) and Francis Prucha's *American Indian Policy in Crisis* (Norman, OK, 1976). After reading these books one does not have the sense that satisfactory alternatives presented themselves to the reformers. This impression is strengthened when biographies of key Indian reformers are examined. See, for example, Ruth O'Dell's sympathetic *Helen Hunt Jackson* (New York, 1939) or Everett Gilcreast's "Richard Henry Pratt and American Indian Policy 1877–1906: A Study of the Assimilation Movement" (Unpublished Ph.D. dissertation, Yale University, 1967). Francis Prucha had edited a collection of writings by the reformers themselves, *Americanizing the American Indians: Writings by the "Friends of the Indian" 1880–1900* (Cambridge, MA, 1973).

Although the differences between soldiers and civilians on Indian policy often seemed substantial—see Donald J. D'Elia's "The Argument Over Civilian or Military Control, 1865-1880," *The Historian* (1962)—each group usually gave way before what seemed to be ineluctable economic arguments. This point is forcefully made by H. Craig Miner in *The Corporation and the Indian* (Columbia, MO, 1976). The fusion of ideology and economics is assessed in Delos Otis' *The Dawes Act and the Allotment of Indian Lands* (Norman, OK, 1973).

The paucity of materials that illuminate the perceptions and experiences of native Americans certainly limits the historian. In recent years this problem has been addressed by anthropologies and ethnologists. One hopes for more works of the caliber of Anthony F. C. Wallace's *Death and Rebirth of the Seneca* (New York, 1970) and Joseph Jorgensen's *The Sun Dance Religion: Power for the Powerless* (Chicago, 1972).

ETHNICITY

The context of industrialization is crucial to an understanding of the impact of immigration. This argument, made twenty years ago by Samuel Hays in *The Response to Industrialism, 1885-1914* (Chicago, 1957), has influenced most subsequent historians. Robert Wiebe's influential *The Search For Order, 1877-1920* (New York, 1967) argues that a "crisis in the communities" with an attendant breakdown in values, identity, and security influenced the ways middle-class Americans received immigrants. These two books confront most of the key issues faced by immigrants.

The books cited in the text adequately treat the response of the genteel establishment to imigration. John Higham's classic *Strangers in the Land: Patterns of American Nativism, 1865-1925* (New Brunswick, NJ, 1955) should be read first. The book analyzes the relationship between immigrants and all strata of American society. Oscar Handlin's *Race and Nationality in American Life* (Boston, 1948) and *Immigration as a Factor in*

American History (Englewood Cliffs, 1959) are useful supplements. John Sproat's *The Best Men: Liberal Reformers in the Gilded Age* (New York, 1968) treats the wide-ranging discontents of these "querulous aristocrats" who had become increasingly incompatible with their age. John Tomsich's *A Genteel Endeavor* (Stanford, 1971) has much the same theme. Students should pay particular attention to Tomsich's view of the xenophobia of Thomas Bailey Aldrich. Barbara Miller Solomon's *Ancestors and Immigrants* (Cambridge, MA, 1956) deals exclusively with Massachusetts; the Bay State was, after all, the hub of the genteel establishment. Mark Haller's *Eugenics: Hereditarian Attitudes in American Thought* (New Brunswick, NJ, 1963) shows how anti-immigrant animus succored the "science" of eugenics.

The middle-class response to immigration is much more difficult to gauge but should be approached in the context of Wiebe's "search for order." The findings of the "new social history" seem to indicate that "ethnic issues" such as schools, temperance, and blue laws are a significant motive force in political behavior. See, for example, Paul Kleppner's *Cross of Culture: A Social Analysis of Midwestern Politics 1850-1900* (New York, 1970); Richard Jensen's *The Winning of the Midwest: Social and Political Conflict, 1888-1896* (Chicago, 1971); Samuel T. McSeveney's *The Politics of Depression* (New York, 1972). Donald Kinzer's *An Episode in Anti-Catholicism* (Seattle, 1964) reveals the organizational tendencies of xenophobes, although the author admits that the impact of the American Protective Association was minimal.

The schools often became an arena of controversy for immigrants, nativists, and well-intentioned reformers. The best general account of changing patterns in education is Laurence Cremin's *The Transformation of the School: Progressivism in American Education 1876-1957* (New York, 1961). Marvin Lazerson in *Origins of the Urban School* (Cambridge, MA, 1971) indicts reformers for forcing children into a white, Protestant middle-class mode. *Work Without Salvation* (Baltimore, 1977) contains James Gilbert's observations on vocationalism in

American education. Edmund Hartmann gauges the pressure for Americanization during World War I in *The Americanization of the Immigrant* (New York, 1948). Students should compare these books with Timothy Smith's view of education from the immigrants' perspective in "Immigrant Social Aspirations and American Education 1880–1930," *American Quarterly* (1969).

A key source of tension between immigrants and "natives" centered around the impact of the newcomers on the economy. Here, Higham's *Stangers in the Land* is indispensable. Charlotte Erickson's *American Industry and the European Immigrant* (New York, 1957) demonstrates that the issue of contract labor became hopelessly entangled with attempts to keep Europe's "scum" out of the United States. Henry David's *The History of the Haymarket Affair* (New York, 1936) reveals that many Americans thought industrial strife and immigration were inextricably linked. Whether or not workers were organizable is the theme of *The Slavic Community of Strike: Immigrant Labor in Anthracite Pennsylvania* (South Bend, 1968) by Victor Greene and a minor theme of Donald Cole's *Immigrant City* (Chapel Hill, NC, 1963) which deals with the immigrant response to a strike in Lawrence, Massachusetts, in 1912. Gerd Korman's *Industrialism, Immigrants and Americanizers* (Madison, 1967) examines the industrial sponsored Americanization programs of the twentieth century. The aim was clearly to create a more docile labor force. The devasting impact of anti-Oriental sentiment on California workers is discussed in Alexander Saxton's *The Indispensable Enemy: Labor and the Anti-Chinese Movement in California* (Berkeley, 1971). Students who wish to explore the response to Chinese immigration further should consult Stuart C. Miller's *The Unwelcome Immigrant: American Images of the Chinese 1785–1882* (Berkeley, 1969).

Discussions of immigration and the economy often include the relationship between immigrant workers and socialism. Historians have sought to explain the failure of socialism in part by examining the geographic mobility of the newcomers and the difficulty of attracting disparate ethnic groups to a unified movement. David Shannon in *The Socialist Party of America* (New York, 1955) discusses the conflicts of ethnic and class allegiance. Yet Abraham Menes argues that socialism reinforced Jewish traditions by stressing group study and historical mission, in "The East Side and the Jewish Labor Movement," *Voices From the Yiddish,* Irving Howe and Eliezer Greenberg, eds. (Ann Arbor, 1972). Howe addresses some of these issues in *The World of Our Fathers* (New York, 1976). Gerald Rosenblum in *Immigrant Workers: Their Impact on American Labor Radicalism* (New York, 1973) explains that immigrants were reluctant to join a radical movement because they could not "protest previously institutionalized practices they had never experienced." David Brody asserts in *Steelworkers in America: The Nonunion Era* (Cambridge, MA, 1960) that before World War I the expectation of a return to Europe convinced immigrants to work long hours for low wages. Of course some immigrants *were* radicals. Melvyn Dubofsky's *We Shall Be All* (Chicago, 1969) notes the immigrant ranks of the Industrial Workers of the World. William Leuchtenberg's *The Perils of Prosperity* (Chicago, 1958) and Robert K. Murray's *Red Scare, A Study in National Hysteria, 1919-1920* (Minneapolis, 1955) examine the treatment of immigrants suspected of disloyalty and/or radicalism during and after the war. Students of labor, radicalism, and immigration should read Daniel Rodger's *The Work Ethic in Industrial America 1850-1920* (Chicago, 1978), a superb analysis of the meaning of work.

Progressivism was so diverse a "movement" that a search for *the* attitude of progressives toward immigration and ethnicity is certainly futile. Students should consult Allen F. Davis' *Spearheads For Reform* (New York, 1967) and *American Heroine: The Life and Legend of Jane Addams* (New York, 1973) for the relationship of settlement workers and immigrants. Another view is advanced by Christopher Lasch in *The New Radicalism in America, 1889-1963* (New York, 1967). Key interpretations of various strands of progressivism include Richard Hofstadter's *The Age of Reform* (New York, 1955); Roger Daniels' *The Politics of Prejudice* (Los Angeles, 1962); Roy Lubove's *The Pro-*

gressive and the Slums (Pittsburgh, 1963); George Mowry's *The Era of Theodore Roosevelt, 1900-1912* (New York, 1958) and *The California Progressives* (Berkeley, 1951); and Arthur S. Link's *The New Freedom* (Princeton, 1956). The alliance between immigrants and urban bosses certainly disturbed many progressives. This theme is examined by Elmer Cornwell in "Bosses, Machines and Ethnic Groups," *Annals of the American Academy of Political and Social Science* (1964). John Buenker in *Urban Liberalism and Progressive Reform* (New York, 1973) insists that the machines were often receptive to progressive reforms. Pluralists like Kallen and Bourne matured as progressives and owed much to the philosophy of pragmatism. For an excellent critique of Kallen see John Higham's *Send These To Me: Jews and Other Immigrants in Urban America* (New York, 1975). Morton White's *Social Thought in America: The Revolt Against Formalism* (New York, 1949) and Philip Wiener's *Evolution and the Founders of Pragmatism* are superior introductions to pragmatist thought but do not make explicit connections between pragmatism and pluralism. Randolph Bourne's *War and the Intellectuals,* Carl Resek, ed. (New York, 1964) provides indispensable insights on this theme.

The focus of historians in the last decade has shifted to the immigrants themselves. In large measure historians have followed the lead of racial and ethnic chauvinists who have rediscovered their "roots." In *Ethnicity: Theory and Experience* (Cambridge, MA, 1975), Nathan Glazer and Daniel P. Moynihan point to a pronounced and sudden increase by people to insist on the significance of their group distinctiveness and identity. The authors helped fuel this tendency in *Beyond the Melting Pot* (Cambridge, MA, 1963). Another key spokesman of ineffable ethnicity is Michael Novak, *The Rise of the Unmeltable Ethnics* (New York, 1974). These works should be contrasted with Milton Gordon's *Assimilation in American Life* (New York, 1964) and Will Herberg's *Protestant Catholic Jew* (Garden City, 1956). A useful source book is edited by Stanley Feldstein and Lawrence Costello, *The Ordeal of Assimilation* (New York, 1974).

Before this explosion of ethnic consciousness, historians usually explored immigration in terms set down by Oscar Handlin. In a number of influential works, most notably *Boston's Immigrants* (Cambridge, MA, 1941) and *The Uprooted* (New York, 1951), Handlin chronicled the anguish of peasant peoples "uprooted" and transferred to urban industrial America. Critics in recent years have faulted Handlin for stereotyping immigrants as peasants and for undervaluing the persistence of ethnicity. Rudolph Vecoli has led the attack in "Contadini in Chicago," *Journal of American History* (1964); "Prelates and Peasants: Italian Immigrants and the Catholic Church," *Journal of Social History* (1969); "European Americans: From Immigrants to Ethnics," in *The Reinterpretation of American History and Culture,* William H. Cartwright and Richard L. Watson Jr., eds. (Washington, 1973). Virginia Yans-McLaughlin in *Family and Community: Italian Immigrants in Buffalo, 1880–1930* (Ithaca, NY, 1977) stresses the strength of immigrant families. Victor Greene in *For God and Country: The Rise of Polish and Lithuanian Ethnic Consciousness in America 1860–1910* (Madison, 1975) and Richard Linkh in *American Catholicism and European Immigrants* (Staten Island, 1975) assess the strength and durability of immigrant nationalism and religious beliefs. Other useful accounts of the immigrant experience include Howe's *The World of Our Fathers;* Moses Rischin's *The Promised City: New York's Jews, 1870–1914* (Cambridge, MA, 1962); Humbert Nelli's *The Italians in Chicago, 1880–1930* (New York, 1970); Thomas Kessner's *The Golden Door: Italian and Jewish Immigrant Mobility in New York City, 1880–1915* (New York, 1977); and Rowland Berthoff's *British Immigrants in Industrial America, 1790–1950* (Cambridge, MA, 1953). The essays in Melvin G. Holli and Peter d'A. Jones, eds., *The Ethnic Frontier* (Grand Rapids, MI, 1977) explore immigrant cultures. Ethnic consciousness, it should be added, has followed in the wake of race consciousness. For a recent example see Herbert Gutman's *The Black Family in Slavery and Freedom, 1750–1925* (New York, 1976).

For a view that stresses immigrant receptivity to some forms of acculturation see Timothy Smith's "Religion and Ethnicity in America," *American Historical Review* (1978); and also "Religious Denominations as Ethnic Communities," *Church History* (1966). Smith's student John Briggs, in *An Italian Passage: Immigrants to Three American Cities, 1890-1930* (New Haven, 1978), has also explored this theme. Two books, finally, that provide the most insights into the immigrant perspective are Herbert Gutman's splendid *Work Culture and Society* (New York, 1975) and John Higham's lucid and balanced *Send These To Me: Jews and Other Immigrants in Urban America* (New York, 1975).

CLASS

Many Americans, I have argued, conflated race, ethnicity, and class. They saw most non-Anglo-Saxon Protestants as members of alien races. Most of the books cited above contain evidence that fears of class conflict accompanied concern about the Negro problem, ethnic pollution, and industrial violence. The reader should also consult Paul Boller Jr.'s *American Thought in Transition: The Impact of Evolutionary Naturalism, 1865-1900* (Chicago, 1969), which briefly analyzes most of the major thinkers of the era.

Nineteenth-century reformers viewed working class poverty as a moral problem. Paul Boyer's brilliant *Urban Masses and Moral Order in America, 1820-1920* (Cambridge, MA, 1978) examines their mixed motives: sympathy, social control, a spiritual impulse to cement the classes. Robert Bremner in *From the Depths: The Discovery of Poverty in the United States* (New York, 1956) explores the heightened consciences of intellectuals and artists. Two useful books more limited in scope are Carroll Smith Rosenberg's *Religion and the Rise of the American City* (Ithaca, NY, 1971) and Paul Ringenbach's *Tramps and Reformers, 1873-1916* (Westport, CT, 1973). Reformers supported their moral explanation of poverty with assertions that economic mobility in America was limitless. Irvin Wyllie in *The*

Self-Made Man in America (New Brunswick, NJ, 1954) and John Cawelti in *Apostles of the Self-Made Man* (Chicago, 1965) examine this pervasive theme in American thought. Richard Weiss, in "Horatio Alger Jr. and the Response to Industrialism," *The Age of Industrialism in America,* Frederick Jaher, ed. (New York, 1968), attempts to account for the popularity of the Alger myth. Social historians in the past decade have sought to measure mobility in the United States. Students should begin with Herbert Gutman's provoctive essay "The Reality of the Rags to Riches 'Myth,'" in *Work, Culture and Society* (New York, 1975).

Social Darwinists sometimes criticized class cooperation because it hindered the survival of the fittest. The relationship between Social Darwinism and laissez-faire economics is examined by Robert McCloskey in *American Conservatism in the Age of Enterprise, 1865–1910* (Cambridge, MA, 1951) and Edward Kirkland in *Dream and Thought in the Business Community, 1860–1900* (Ithaca, NY, 1956). Richard Hofstadter's classic *Social Darwinism in American Though* (Philadelphia, 1945) remains the best book on this subject although it overstates the influence of Social Darwinism in America. Hofstadter argues that Darwinism had a "dual potential" that made it serviceable for thinkers as diverse as William Graham Sumner and Lester Frank Ward. Cynthia Russett's less original *Darwin in America: the Intellectual Response, 1865–1912* (San Francisco, 1976) analyzes some thinkers ignored by Hofstadter.

The fear of class conflict grew in proportion to increases in immigration and industrialization. Frederic Jaher has pulled together several nightmare visions from literature in *Doubters and Dissenters: Cataclysmic Thought in America* (London, 1964). Yet Jaher's "paranoids" had their counterparts among the more respected members of American society. Henry May in *The Protestant Churches and Industrial America* (New York, 1949) and Aaron Abell in *The Urban Impact on American Protestantism 1865–1900* (Cambridge, MA, 1943) gauge the anxiety of clergymen about class conflagration sparked by such ominous events as the Haymarket Affair. Paul Meyer in "The Fear of

Cultural Decline: Josiah Strong's Thoughts About Reform and Expansion," *Church History* (1973), views Strong in this context. Walter LaFeber's *The New Empire: An Interpretation of American Expansion 1860-1898* (Ithaca, NY, 1963) compares Strong, Frederick Jackson Turner, and Admiral Mahan. American writers increasingly used class as a theme. Jay Martin's *Harvests of Change: American Literature, 1865-1914* (Englewood Cliffs, 1967) provides a thorough analysis of literary trends and contrasts as, for example, Stephen Crane's "A Night at the Millionaire's Club" with his treatment of the brutalized working class in "In the Depths of the Coal Mine." *The Ferment of Realism: American Literature, 1884-1919* (New York, 1965) by Warner Berthoff effectively complements Martin. Readers should compare the "paralyzing environmentalism" of the naturalism of Frank Norris with the "positive environmentalism" of twentieth-century progressive social thinkers. Larzer Ziff in *The American 1890's* (New York, 1966) examines *fin du siecle* literature as does Everett Carter in *Howells and the Age of Realism* (Philadelphia, 1954).

The desire to ease or eliminate class antagonisms motivated reformers and utopian writers. Daniel Aaron's *Men of Good Hope: A Story of American Progressives* (New York, 1951) provides a suitable introduction to George, Bellamy, Howells, Veblen, and Henry Demarest Lloyd. Charles Barker's encyclopedic *Henry George* (New York, 1955) assesses the program of the Single Taxer. Sylvia Bowman in *the Year 2000: A Critical Biography of Edward Bellamy* (New York, 1958) adequately reviews Bellamy's career. a recent though not entirely satisfactory attempt to analyze utopian literature is Kenneth Roemers' *The Obsolete Necessity: America in Utopian Writing, 1888-1900* (Kent, OH, 1976). The Populists often anguished about class as well as race. While Richard Hofstadter in *The Age of Reform* (New York, 1956) argued that the Populists were middle-class entrepreneurs who often posed as injured yeomen, Lawrence Goodwyn in *Democratic Promise* (New York, 1976) has persuasively documented the powerful radical dimensions of populism. Norman Pollack's *The Populist Response to In-*

dustrial America (Cambridge, MA, 1962) attacks the contention that the populists were "backward-looking" and stresses the ambitious attempt, spearheaded by Henry D. Lloyd, to construct an alliance between farmers and urban workers.

Accounts of socialism in the United States invariably attempt to explain the failure of radicalism. The interested student should begin with Howard Quint's *The Forging of American Socialism* (2d ed. Indianapolis, 1964) which concludes with the birth of a united Socialist Party in 1900, and David Shannon's *The Socialist Party of America* (Chicago, 1967) which focuses on twentieth-century developments. Daniel Bell's *Marxian Socialism in the United States* (Princeton, 1967) advances several reasons for the failure to develop revolutionary class consciousness in the United States. Happily, Werner Sombart's *Why Is There No Socialism in the United States?*, translated by Patricia M. Hocking and C. T. Husbands (White Plains, NY, 1976), has at long last been published in English. Sombart's insights remain invaluable. Henry Bedford's *Socialism and Workers in Massachusetts, 1886–1912* (Amherst, 1966) and Ira Kipnis' *The American Socialist Movement, 1879–1912* (New York, 1952) examine socialism at the height of its power. James Weinstein in *The Decline of Socialism in America, 1912–1925* (New York, 1967) makes the revisionist argument that the strength of socialism actually increased during World War I. Two fine biographies of American radicals are Ray Ginger's *The Bending Cross: A Biography of Eugene Victor Debs* (New Brunswick, NJ, 1949) and L. Glen Seretan's *Daniel DeLeon: The Odyssey of An American Marxist* (Cambridge, MA, 1978).

Explanations of the failure of socialism inevitably focus upon the labor movement. Indeed "the road not taken" by American workers informs, even haunts, labor history. Selig Perlman's *A Theory of the Labor Movement* (New York, 1928) is a fine introduction to this subject. The book should be read in tandem with Norman Ware's still useful *The Labor Movement in the United States, 1860–1895* (New York, 1929). Gerald Grob in *Workers and Utopia: A Study of Ideological Conflict in the American Labor Movement, 1865–1900* (Evanston, IL, 1961) argues that the Knights of Labor failed because it was dominated by the preindustrial utopian ethos of antebellum reform. Grob contrasts the Knights' difficulties to the successful "realism" of Samuel Gompers and the American Federation of Labor. The same theme informs Harold Livesay's *Samuel Gompers and Organized Labor in America* (Boston, 1978). For a discussion of the complex response of progressives to the labor question see Irwin Yellowitz' *Labor and the Progressive Movement in New York State, 1897–1916* (Ithaca, NY, 1965). For more than a decade Herbert Gutman has criticized the exclusive focus of labor historians on unions. Most workers were not organized. Gutman's *Work, Culture and Society* (New York, 1975) examines the response to industrialism of workers and gauges the reactions of the communities in which they lived. Daniel Rodgers in *The Work Ethic in Industrial America, 1850–1920* (Chicago, 1978) takes Gutman's advice and gets labor history out of a narrowly institutional setting. The response of businessmen to the demands of industrial labor is analyzed by Samuel Haber in *Efficiency and Uplift: Scientific Management in the Progressive Era, 1890–1920* (Chicago, 1964). The book contains an illuminating analysis of Frederick W. Taylor. A somewhat less successful treatment of the same subject is Loren Baritz' *Servants of Power: A History of the Use of Social Science in American Industry* (Middletown, CT, 1960).

The emergence of social scientists and social engineers in the late nineteenth century is integral to an understanding of progressivism and the growth of the modern liberal state. Recent studies of this phenomenon shed great light upon the progressives' views of social structure and the morphology of change. Thomas Haskell's brilliant *The Emergence of Professional Social Science* (Urbana, IL, 1978) contrasts the positive environmentalism of social scientists with earlier and more ennervating forms of environmental determinism. Mary O. Furner in *Advocacy and Objectivity* (Lexington, KY 1975) explores the dilemma of social scientists: should they merely gather the "facts" or become knights on a reform quest? Burton Bledstein in *The Culture of Professionalism: The Middle Class and the*

Development of Higher Education in America (New York, 1976) looks at educators as shapers and reflecters of American values. Two fine studies of the social scientists' quest for community are Jean Quandt's *From the Small Town to the Great Community* (New Brunswick, NJ, 1970) and R. Jackson Wilson's *In Quest of Community: Social Philosophy in the United States, 1860–1920* (New York, 1968). Wilson's analysis of E. A. Ross, James Mark Baldwin, and Josiah Royce should be seen as an ideological ambiance for Paul Boyer's discussion of the concept of civic loyalty in *Urban Masses and Moral Order in America* (Cambridge, MA, 1978). Of all the social scientists, economists probably had the greatest impact upon American society. Sidney Fine in *Laissez-Faire and the General Welfare State* (Ann Arbor, 1956) sees modern liberalism as a compromise between socialism and laissez faire. Virtually all of the "new economists" received their training in Germany. They returned to the United States with a different view of the role of the state. Joseph Dorfman in "The Role of the German Historical School in American Economic Thought," *The American Economic Review* (1955), and Jergen Herbst in *The German Historical School in American Scholarship* (Ithaca, NY, 1965) examine the transformation of economic theory. The same theme is examined through biography: Benjamin Rader's *The Academic Mind and Reform: The Influence of Richard T. Ely in American Life* (Lexington, KY, 1966) and Daniel M. Fox' *The Discovery of Abundance: Simon N. Patten and the Transformation of Social Theory* (Ithaca, NY, 1967). I have learned from Fox that progressives used the notion of abundance generated from a reformed industrial capitalism to argue that radical change was unnecessary. John P. Diggins in *The Bard of Savagery: Thorstein Veblen and Modern Social Theory* (New York, 1978) compares Veblen with Marx and Weber.

Many progressives sought to bridge the gap between theory and practice by bringing social scientists into government and by applying social science techniques to social problems. The "praxis" of progressives is examined in Roy Lubove's *The Professional Altruist: The Emergence of Social Work as a Career*

(Cambridge, MA, 1965) and Anthony Platt's *The Child Savers: The Invention of Delinquency* (Chicago, 1969). The aims of progressives that underlay these efforts are analyzed in Don Kirschner's "The Ambiguous Legacy: Social Justice and Social Control in the Progressive Era," *Historical Reflections* (1975). Kirschner focuses on such innovations as the neighborhood center and stresses the positive environmentalism of progressives. Kenneth McNaught in "American Progressives and the Good Society," *Journal of American History* (1966), and Kenneth Kusmer in "The Functions of Organized Charity in the Progressive Era: Chicago as a Case Study," *Journal of American History* (1973), have different views of the fundamental goals of the progressives. In "Social Tensions and the Origin of Progressivism," *Journal of American History* (1969), David Thelen provocatively proposes that the depression of the 1890s paradoxically ushered in progressivism by weakening class allegiances. Formerly discrete social groups could then unite under the banner of cooperation and the public interest. The relationship between American Protestantism and progressivism is important to an understanding of reform. The standard work on the Social Gospel is Charles Howard Hopkins' *The Rise of the Social Gospel in American Protestantism, 1860–1915* (New Haven, 1940). David Noble places Walter Rauschenbusch in the context of progressivism in *The Paradox of Progressive Thought* (Minneapolis, 1958).

The degree to which progressives accepted collectivism and the corporation has long stirred historical controversy. Three revisionist historians who argue that progressivism was a severely limited movement (and who lament the road not taken by progressives) are James Gilbert, *Designing the Industrial State* (Chicago, 1972); Gabriel Kolko, *The Triumph of Conservatism* (New York, 1963); and James Weinstein, *The Corporate Ideal in the Liberal State, 1900–1918* (Boston, 1968). These books should be compared with Arthur S. Link's *The New Freedom* (Princeton, 1956) and Charles Forcey's *The Crossroads of Liberalism* (New York, 1961).

The progressives' use of the concept of loyalty is superbly delineated by Boyer, Quandt, and R. Jackson Wilson. Useful supplements include Thomas Hines' *Burnham of Chicago, Architect and Planner* (New York, 1974); Geoffrey Blodgett's "Frederick Law Olmstead: Landscape Architecture as Conservative Reform," *Journal of American History* (1976); and Harvey Kantor's "The City Beautiful in New York," *New York Historical Society Quarterly* (1973). Blaine Brownell examines civic loyalty in debased form in *The Urban Ethos in the South, 1920–1930* (Baton Rouge, 1975).

Finally, those interested in the fate of progressivism in the 1920s should consult Arthur S. Link's "What Happened to the Progressive Movement in the 1920's?" *American Historical Review* (1959).

INDEX